WHEN WORDS TRUMP POLITICS

WHEN WORDS TRUMP POLITICS

Resisting a Hostile Regime of Language

ADAM HODGES

stanford briefs
An Imprint of Stanford University Press
Stanford, California

Stanford University Press
Stanford, California

Printed in the United States of America
on acid-free, archival-quality paper

Library of Congress Cataloging-in-Publication Data is available
upon request from the Library of Congress

Library of Congress Control Number:2019948788

Cover design: Rob Ehle

Typeset by Classic Typography in 11/15 Adobe Garamond

CONTENTS

PREFACE

Today, a nation ringed by walls would only imprison itself.

—Barack Obama[1]

As often happens with events of historical importance, people are not likely to forget where they were when the 2016 presidential election was called for Donald Trump. Trump was an unlikely candidate who many, including on his own team, didn't expect to actually win the presidency. According to news reports, he either didn't have a victory speech prepared or had only a rough draft that his team had to hastily revise once the election results went his way. Meanwhile, collective shock set in among those who had been lulled by polls into believing that Hillary Clinton would become the first woman president.

I voted by absentee ballot since I was teaching overseas at Carnegie Mellon University's international campus in Doha, Qatar. The campus is home to students of around 40 different nationalities. These students, a majority of them Muslims, gathered on this global campus to pursue an American university education while remaining closer to family and home.

I woke up early Wednesday morning, November 9, 2016, to start my day and head to campus. It was still Tuesday evening, election night, in the United States. I turned on CNN International to get a glimpse of the preliminary results and saw a sea of red on the national electoral map. Within a few hours, media outlets called the election in favor of Donald Trump.

The day after learning the news, our student government held its weekly *majlis* (Arabic for "assembly"). Usually, it's a time for students to socialize and hold extracurricular activities related to university life. But this week the majlis featured a panel of professors who attempted to answer student questions about how a man who pledged "a total and complete shutdown of Muslims entering the United States" could actually be elected US president. What would that mean for our Muslim students who planned to spend a semester studying at our home campus in the United States? Would they still be allowed to do so? If so, would they be welcomed or treated in ways suggested by Trump's anti-Muslim rhetoric?

Trump's rhetoric on the campaign trail may have targeted an American audience, but it was heard around the world. His antiglobalist stance belies the reality of the interconnected world of the 21st century. No physical border wall can stop the informational, technological, and cultural flows that rapidly circle the globe and bring us all closer together. But metaphorical walls—built on ignorance and divisive rhetoric—can prevent us from recognizing our common humanity and working together to respond effectively to the global challenges we face.

Trump's election would not bode well for the future if the worst of his campaign rhetoric was converted into policy. But on the positive side, many thought, partisan candidates who assume the presidency often shift toward a more united stance as they attempt to bring people together and govern pragmatically. The gravitas of the office eventually takes hold and shapes them into better leaders by virtue of necessity. Such hope proved fleeting in this case. Any hope that Trump's rhetorical threats would subside once he took office was dispelled a week after his inauguration when he instituted his "Muslim ban" as an executive order. That would prove to be the beginning of a long series of policies built on the divisive rhetoric of the campaign trail. And the tweets kept coming.

Trump's penchant for showmanship and his incessant use of Twitter provided a never-ending stream of material to write about. Inevitably, Trump would say—or tweet—something that formed the seed for another essay found in this book. These essays are an attempt to better understand the communicative dimensions of Trumpian politics, a type of politics that goes beyond Trump to encompass a reactionary tide of right-wing populisms that has swept around the world from Hungary to Brazil. My aim is to analyze these politics, from a discourse-centered perspective, without inadvertently feeding them and with implications for how to counter the deceptive appeal of the Trump-style rhetor. This book is for those interested in political discourse. Although I apply scholarly ideas in the analyses, no prior specialized knowledge is needed. The book is written for a wide audience—for the general public as well as scholars and students—to offer insights into how Americans, particularly journalists and politicians, can successfully respond to the spell of demagoguery.

Each section in this book includes a set of essays that share a common thematic focus. How do we effectively respond to a cyberbully in the Oval Office? Answer: we untangle his tweets from newsworthy messages and adopt strategies for countering bullying behavior (section 1). How do we make sense of populist movements in a post-truth era? We recognize what makes Trump's brand of populism a form of demagoguery and call out the factually challenged language that underpins it (section 2). How do we explain the spectacle of Trumpian politics? We distinguish between the entertainment value and truth value of political stagecraft and identify the performative core of Trump's message (section 3). How do we hold politicians like Trump accountable for detestable statements and actions? We decode the linguistic moves they use to claim plausible deniability and we reject the specious claims they use to shirk responsibility (section 4). How do we unwittingly avoid spreading "fake news," conspiracy theories, and propaganda? We understand how misinformation propagates on social media and correct the record without inadvertently strengthening false claims (sections 5 and 6). How do we resist Trumpism's Islamophobia and racism? We acknowledge how Trumpian rhetoric demonizes an entire religion and minimizes the existence of racism (sections 7 and 8). How do we resist Trump's divisive politics? We rethink the nature and importance of argumentation in politics and consider some resistance tactics from the #MeToo and silent protest movements (section 9). How do we prevent the Trumpification of the judiciary? We understand how language ideologies help rationalize conservative judicial philosophies and we recognize how Trump's virulent strain of polemics and belligerent masculinity corrodes US institutions like the Supreme Court (section 10). And finally, how do we move beyond Trump? We realize that communicating with him is like communicating with a troll and identify what it will take to successfully run against him (section 11).

Democratic theorists and civic-minded citizens have long emphasized the need for an informed electorate. But being informed on political issues also demands a keen awareness of the way language is used to convey, discuss, debate, and contest those issues. A critical awareness of political discourse can disarm the spurious appeal of the populist demagogue or inspire appropriate responses that seek to unify rather than divide, uplift rather than tear down. This book is an effort to promote intelligent debate on these issues and move our national conversation beyond the politics of division and hate that has marked this time. I encourage readers to apply the ideas and analytic tools they find here to future debates and political campaigns, and help usher in a new era of politics focused on bringing people together to build a better world.

WHEN WORDS TRUMP POLITICS

1 THE CYBERBULLY-IN-CHIEF

If there's one thing that Trump's supporters and critics both agree on, it may very well be that he needs to tweet less. Many of Trump's Republican colleagues in Congress have lamented the fact that his tweets are "not helpful." Even as his tweets rally his base of core supporters, others who voted for him claim to have done so despite the disparaging remarks that emanate from his Twitter feed. Regardless, Trump's loud tweets have come to define his persona and have become an integral part of his political brand.

So how should the public respond to a commander-in-chief who is also the nation's chief cyberbully? The essays in this section suggest we start by untangling his predictable insult-laden tweets from newsworthy messages and follow the advice of the US Department of Health and Human Services website StopBullying.gov for dealing with bullying behavior. Using the presidency to bully journalists, government officials, Gold Star family members, and even deceased senators is a far cry from how President

Theodore Roosevelt used the power of the presidency as a "bully pulpit" to draw attention to issues, mobilize support, and lead the nation. Republican leaders and the rest of US society need to keep this historical context in mind when evaluating how the 45th president (or any president) uses—or abuses—the presidential platform.

TRUMP'S FORMULAIC
TWITTER INSULTS

Every presidential transition also involves a change in the regime of language. On January 20, 2017, the juxtaposition between the outgoing and incoming regimes was especially stark, something President Obama's evening farewell address followed by president-elect Trump's press conference the next morning vividly depicted. However, underlying their many obvious differences is the common rhetorical device of repetition—Obama to inspire and affirm shared values, Trump to peddle insults peppered with gratuitous modifiers.[1]

In his farewell address, Obama demonstrated his familiar composure, marked by effective use of timing, repetition, and storytelling, a style well documented by Geneva Smitherman and H. Samy Alim in their book *Articulate While Black*.[2] The next morning, Trump demonstrated his own style, marked by visual excess and hyperbole.[3] A stack of manila folders on the table next to the podium, which Trump theatrically pointed to as evidence—visible, physical evidence—of his efforts to distance himself from business interests, epitomizes that visually oriented, gesturally rich style.

Presidential styles personify characters from American life. If George W. Bush was the cowboy and Barack Obama the professor, then it seems Donald J. Trump is the school-yard bully or, to be slightly more generous, the American snake-oil salesman. Out goes the orator-in-chief and in comes the entertainer-in-chief. Yet as anthropologists like Kira Hall, Donna M. Goldstein, and Matthew Bruce Ingram implore us to consider, merely studying the eco-nomical, sociological, and psychological dimensions of Trump's appeal while ignoring the discursive elements of this new language regime will yield an incomplete under-standing of what makes Trump's spectacular show so com-pellingly pleasing, or offensive.[4]

On the surface—and let's be honest, from the perspec-tive of the intellectual elite that serves as the foil to Trump's populism—the styles of Trump and Obama seem to have little in common. Intellectuals love Obama in large part because he talks and acts like one of them. He's a law professor who provides carefully considered state-ments marked by coherence, cohesion, and nuance. He embodies the rhetorical style taught in every first-year col-lege writing class. In contrast, Trump is the first-year stu-dent who can't seem to provide a coherent answer to the essay prompt.

Yet both draw on the common rhetorical device of rep-etition within and across speech events, even as they implement this device in different ways and to different ends. Obama excels at this, as evidenced by the inspira-tional "Yes, We Can" slogan used throughout his cam-paign and revisited in his farewell address.[5] Trump also excels in his command of this rhetorical device, as evidenced by his use of repetition in his large corpus of derogatory tweets.

A few weeks before the November 2016 election, the *New York Times* published a complete list of "The 282 People, Places and Things Donald Trump Has Insulted on Twitter." Of course, it didn't take long for the list to become incomplete. At the time of his inauguration, the list included 289 people, places, and things; and two years into his presidency the list had grown to 551 and counting.[6] The *Times* actually began tabulating the insults in January 2016 after culling through and categorizing over 4,000 tweets Trump made since he launched his presidential bid in June 2015. When the project first launched, the *Times* reported it had "found that one in every eight [tweets] was a personal insult of some kind." As of the time of Trump's inauguration, the list contained 2,268 discrete quotes.

These tweets provide insight into the regime of language ushered in with the Trump presidency. Insults, by their very nature, accord with the schoolyard bully persona, but these tweets also epitomize the rhetorical moves of the snake-oil salesman—the language of advertising at its slimiest. Trump summarizes these moves through the words of his ghostwriter in his book *The Art of the Deal*: "I play to people's fantasies. . . . People want to believe that something is the biggest and the greatest and the most spectacular. I call it truthful hyperbole. It's an innocent form of exaggeration—and it's a very effective form of promotion."[7]

Indeed, the list of Trump's tweets compiled by the *Times* is rife with hyperbole and exaggeration. He achieves this through the use of repetition of gratuitous modifiers and intensifiers. Here's the formula. Start with a small set of nouns. Trump's favorites include *clown, disaster, dope, dummy, joke, liar.* Next, layer on the hyperbole and exaggeration by adding a needless modifier. Notably, adjectives far outnumber nouns in the list. Contrary to William Strunk's advice to writers to use adjectives sparingly, snake-oil salesmen must pile on the modifiers to punctuate the emotional appeal. Trump's preferred adjectives range from *absolute* to *zero.* In between are *bad, biased, boring, corrupt, crazy, crooked, disgraceful, disgusting, dumb, failed, failing, false . . . incapable, incompetent, ineffective . . .* and, of course, *sad, stupid, terrible, weak.*

Mikhail Bakhtin, in *The Dialogic Imagination,* underscores the compulsion to repeat that underlies all language use.[8] Instead of linguistic creativity yielding unbridled variation, we typically make use of limited variations on a common theme. Trump's tweets illustrate this variation-on-a-theme approach. Take, for example, one of his most frequently used nouns: *disaster.* Variation occurs around this theme through the use of modifiers to produce insults such as "a complete disaster," "a total disaster," "a horrible disaster," "a foreign policy disaster," "a formula for disaster." You get the point.

The final step is to sprinkle intensifiers—semantically vacuous adverbs—over the message to enhance its emotional impact. Trump's most often tweeted intensifiers are (in order of popularity) *very, totally, so, really*. He also likes *100%* as an intensifier, as in "100% fabricated," "100% made up," "100% owned by her donors," "100% CONTROLLED" (with ALL CAPS used to amplify the volume of the message). Using this formula, we might anticipate a Trumpian retort to this writer's essay in 140 characters: "Biased and 100% irrelevant. Has zero credibility. Written by a failing dopey writer. Knows NOTHING! What a clown. Don't read #WhenWordsTrumpPolitics."

Although it may be tempting to adopt Trump's own formula to wage stinging counterattacks, the real value of knowing the formula is to enable our mental spam filters to discriminate between lazy polemics and newsworthy messages. Trump's formulaic Twitter insults are agents of mass distraction that merely deflect our attention and divide our efforts to prevent the implementation of his worst policies.

HOW TO TWEET LIKE TRUMP

Take a derogatory noun.

Add a gratuitous modifier.

Sprinkle with vacuous intensifiers.

Repeat.

In her book *The Bully Pulpit*, historian Doris Kearns Goodwin examines Theodore Roosevelt's leadership during his time as president.[9] She argues that in successfully working to enact progressive reforms, Roosevelt created "a new kind of presidency and a new vision of the relationship between the government and the people." Central to that leadership was Roosevelt's mastery of the "bully pulpit." Defined today as *a public office or position of authority that provides its occupant with an outstanding opportunity to speak out on any issue,* the term itself was coined by Roosevelt, Goodwin explains, "to describe the national platform the presidency provides to shape public sentiment and mobilize action."[10]

In American vernacular of the day, *bully* (as an adjective) meant "very good; first-rate." Combined with *pulpit,* or a speaking platform, Roosevelt used the term to refer to the power that the presidency gave him to speak and be heard on vital issues facing the nation, from labor rights to political corruption to consumer food and drug safety. From Roosevelt onward, American presidents employed the presidential bully pulpit to advocate and promote their political agendas. But under the presidency of Donald Trump, the advocacy-oriented bully pulpit as originally conceived by Roosevelt has morphed into a crude platform to engage in bullying behavior.

Bully (as a noun) refers to someone who uses their strength or power to harm or intimidate those who are weaker. The power imbalance between a bully and their prey is a key element of bullying behavior. As defined by StopBullying.gov, an educational website run by the US Department of Health and Human Services, "Bullying is unwanted, aggressive behavior among school aged children that involves a real or perceived power imbalance. The behavior is repeated, or has the potential to be repeated, over time." Oftentimes, the behavior moves into the realm of *cyberbullying*, or the use of electronic communication to bully a person, typically by sending messages of an intimidating or threatening nature.

The government's own definition is telling when applied to the commander-in-chief. *Unwanted, aggressive behavior.* Check. *Involves a real or perceived power imbalance.* Check. *Repeated over time.* Check. Trump's tweets could be textbook case studies of bullying even if he is a grown man in his 70s and not a school-aged child.

It is bad enough that, reserving much of his vitriol for journalists, Trump has tweeted that the media is "the enemy of the American people" and frequently takes to Twitter to brand unfavorable press coverage as "Fake Media" or "Fake News." But many of his Twitter tirades exhibit ad hominem attacks that cross well into the territory of bullying behavior against journalists, politicians,

and citizens alike—from Alicia Machado to Serge Kovaleski to Megan Kelly to Mika Brzezinski and on and on.
His bullying, personal attacks have continued unabated
despite the hope expressed by many that the presidency
would change the man for the better, making him more
"presidential."

Ironically enough against the backdrop of Trump's
cyberbullying, Melania Trump made a preinauguration
announcement that she would take up the issue of cyberbullying as First Lady—a project that would unfortu-
nately have little impact on the cyberbully in the Oval
Office. If there was any hope that the First Lady could do
some good in combatting cyberbullying, let alone stage an
intervention into her own husband's bullying ways, that
hope faded after Trump took to Twitter to go after the
cohosts of MSNBC's *Morning Joe* show in June 2017. He
started by referring to Joe Scarborough as "Psycho Joe"
and Mika Brzezinski as "low I.Q. Crazy Mika." Then,
reminiscent of Trump's misogynistic comments about
Megan Kelly during the 2016 campaign, he continued to
insult Brzezinski in a follow-up tweet. In response, the
First Lady's communications director released a statement
that defended her husband's tweets about Brzezinski. In
addition, Sarah Huckabee Sanders, at that time the deputy press secretary, further justified the president's tweets
by claiming it was an appropriate way for him to fight
back against critics.

Let's be perfectly clear. There is a definite distinction
between a president who fights back against critics with

bona fide political arguments, and a person who uses the presidential bully pulpit to engage in aggressive personal attacks that seek to harm or intimidate. The former is presidential behavior that engages with the issues; the latter is bullying behavior that shifts attention from the issues because the person either lacks an adequate intellectual response or does not care to craft one.

Part of the problem is that Trump's tweets are too often accepted by his supporters as sufficient arguments rather than the degrading ad hominem attacks that they typically are (thus, Sarah Huckabee Sanders's defense of Trump). Rather than critiquing the message (news coverage) in a way that might raise genuine concerns supported by thoughtful reasons and evidence, Trump's tweets merely insult the messengers (journalists) in an attempt to shift focus from the message.

How should we respond to this hijacking of the presidential bully pulpit? What roles can citizens, journalists, and politicians play to stop the bullying by a man who holds the power of the presidency?

According to StopBullying.gov, "Bullying can be prevented, especially when the power of a community is brought together. Community-wide strategies can help identify and support [those] who are bullied, redirect the behavior of [those] who bully, and change the attitudes of [those] who tolerate bullying behaviors." To stop bullying, the website advises, *Don't ignore it. Intervene immediately. Model respectful behavior when you intervene.* I would emphasize that a community-wide effort in response to

Trump's bullying must involve people and politicians closely allied with him.

Although several Republican lawmakers took to Twitter to respond to Trump's attack on Brzezinski, including Senators Susan Collins, Ben Sasse, Lisa Murkowski, Lindsey Graham, Orin Hatch, and Representative Lynn Jenkins, many others continue to remain silent or provide tepid statements that fail to "send the message that it is not acceptable."[11] Former Arkansas governor Mike Huckabee, for example, called the tweets "a mosquito bite" that should be ignored. But the more this behavior is simply ignored by Trump's most ardent supporters and political allies (even if they silently cringe), the more likely the behavior will continue—much to the detriment of everyone, Republicans included.

Republican leaders should ask, how would President Teddy Roosevelt want them to use their platforms to speak out on this abuse of the presidential bully pulpit? The rest of us should follow the government's own advice to deal with the bully-in-chief.

In *post-truth politics*, the factual accuracy of words and the details of policy weigh less than the ability of words to animate voters. Although post-truth politics is neither new nor unique to Trump, his flagrant disregard for truth is unprecedented among US presidents. A guiding premise of the American experiment in government has been that presidential words need to at least have the pretense of being attached to reality; furthermore, claims should be revised in the face of disconfirming evidence. Even President George W. Bush eventually accepted the reality that there were no weapons of mass destruction in Iraq.

But Trump treats truth as a contrivance. When he uses language to invoke facts and stake out truth claims, what matters most is whether the words seem or feel like they should be true, not whether they actually are true. Comedian Stephen Colbert coined the term *truthiness* to capture the way opinion and intuition can be wielded as facts—"alternative facts"—because those facts (even if disproven or unverifiable) ring true and strike a chord with a preconceived worldview. In many ways, truthiness is just another approach to talking about demagoguery, where policy arguments revolve around claims that are "generally deduced from important in-group values, rather than grounded in falsifiable studies or multipartisan scholarship."[1]

Central to Trump's campaign strategy is the use of prejudicial appeals grounded in a worldview propped up by fabricated stories about Mexicans, Muslims, the "deep state," Robert Mueller's investigative team, and a host of other actors and perceived threats. The essays in this section shed light on the textbook demagoguery of Trump's brand of populism, unpack the metaphors he uses to whip up fear of migrants, and probe how his rhetorical statements adhere to ideological fidelity above factual fidelity. Disarming Trump's fear-based election strategy may start by calling out the spurious foundation upon which that strategy is built.

THE DEMAGOGIC UNDERPINNINGS
OF TRUMP'S POPULISM

All populists champion the ordinary people against an establishment elite, but Trump's brand of populism incorporates elements of demagoguery to conjure up a third scapegoated group that the elite has failed to protect against.

In ancient Greece and Rome, populists were leaders who espoused the cause of the ordinary people, as opposed to the oligarchs (the elite few who ruled in their own interests). The term for these populists was *demagogues* (from the Greek *demos* meaning "the people," and *agogos* "leading"), a term that in modern times has gained a pejorative meaning to designate leaders who use prejudicial appeals rather than rational arguments to mobilize the people.

The term *populism* derives from the Latin root *populus* meaning "the people." In its most basic sense, *populism* refers to political approaches that champion the cause of the ordinary people. Although *populist* can be used in a pejorative manner similar to *demagogue*, it also carries positive connotations when reserved for leaders and movements that give voice to and democratically represent the interests of the people.

But not all populisms are created equal. One need only contrast figures like Bernie Sanders with Donald Trump, or Elizabeth Warren with France's Marine Le Pen, to see that populists span the traditional political spectrum and adopt different strategies to champion the people. If populism is "a language whose speakers conceive of ordinary people as a noble assemblage not bounded narrowly by class; view their elite opponents as self-serving and undemocratic; and seek to mobilize the former against the latter," as historian Michael Kazin defines it,[2] then different populists speak different dialects of populism.

John Judis distinguishes between left-wing and right-wing varieties of populism by pointing out how one is dyadic while the other is triadic. In the dyadic populism of the left, "populists champion the people against an elite or an establishment. Theirs is a vertical politics of the bottom and middle arrayed against the top." In the triadic populism of the right, "populists champion the people against an elite that they accuse of coddling a third group, which can consist, for instance, of immigrants, Islamists, or African American militants."[3] Trump's populism clearly fits the triadic model with both the establishment elite and a third scapegoated group positioned as threats to the ordinary people.

Trump rails against the elite, denouncing not just the "liberal elite" but also an array of "establishment" figures and institutions, from judges (who rule against his administration's policies) to the mainstream media (infamously dubbed "the enemy of the American people") to various career government officials (often sinisterly categorized as "the deep state") and even the Justice Department and FBI (particularly Special Counsel Robert Mueller's team of "angry Democrats" engaged in a "witch hunt").

Trump also demonizes a third group, which represents an ominous threat against which the elites have seemingly failed to protect the ordinary people. The precise identity of the scapegoated group need not remain constant as long as some group is positioned as the third leg of the triad at all times. Mexicans. Muslims. Immigrants. NFL players kneeling during the national anthem. African nations. Syrian refugees. Caravans of asylum-seekers from Central America. The presence of this third group—a constant necessity in the prejudicial appeals of the right-wing populist—turns Trumpism into an invidious form of demagoguery.

Demagoguery polarizes by setting up a simplified binary distinction between "us" (represented by the ordinary people, who are "good") and "them" (represented by the elites and scapegoated out-groups, who are "bad"). Complex issues and policies are reduced to questions of group identity. The acceptability of political arguments comes down to who makes the argument (i.e., which group do they belong to?) rather than the strength of the facts, evidence, and reasoning that support the argument (i.e., what are the merits of their policies?).[4]

The demagogue presents "our" situation as dire and the truth as simple to grasp, while emphasizing the threats that "we" (the ordinary people) face at the hands of the out-groups. This has been a constant since the beginning of Trump's campaign for president when he declared on June 16, 2015, "When Mexico sends its people, they're not sending their best. . . . They're sending people that have lots of problems, and they're bringing those problems with us [*sic*]. They're bringing drugs. They're bringing crime. They're rapists."

Who will deal with the threats to "us"? The elites in the right-wing populist's triad are said to be unable or unwilling to do so effectively. This leaves the demagogue to fill that gap as the sole champion and protector of the people.

In his acceptance speech at the Republican National Convention in July 2016, candidate Trump exclaimed, "Nobody knows the system better than me, which is why I alone can fix it." He went on to claim, "The crime and violence that today afflicts our nation will soon—and I mean very soon—come to an end. Beginning on January 20th 2017, safety will be restored." But the threat can never fully subside for the demagogue because the presence of the threat is an integral pillar in his triadic populism. Trump's demonization of immigrants must continue unabated, picking up renewed vigor before every election. Witness how he exaggerated the "threat" of a migrant caravan of asylum-seekers making its way toward the US-Mexico border in the weeks prior to the 2018 midterm elections.

Of course, a demagogue you disagree with is easy to spot, especially a grifter with a track record of shady business dealings. But demagoguery, as Patricia Roberts-Miller suggests, is not always so obvious to isolate.[5] The problem is that demagoguery has a tendency to spawn more demagoguery as it embeds itself within the political culture and seeps into everyone's discourse. Countering Trumpism, therefore, requires more than simply defeating Trump at the ballot box. It requires advocating for a politics grounded in evidence-based policy deliberations, where arguments rather than the arguers are the center of debate. More like the McCain-Feingold campaign finance reform and less like the healthcare polemics of recent decades.

Trump's immigration metaphors set a divisive tone from the top. He wields demagogic rhetoric like a marketing tool, ramping up prejudicial appeals in the closing days of each election cycle. Chief among his go-to rhetorical devices are immigration metaphors that dehumanize immigrants and militarize policy responses.[6]

Trump's rhetoric includes many of the same immigration metaphors that Otto Santa Ana identified during the 1994 ballot initiative in California—Proposition 187— that would have denied public services to undocumented workers and required mandatory reporting of immigration status by those administering such services.[7] These include the *immigrant as animal* and *immigrant as disease* metaphors, both invoked when Trump tweets that immigrants "infest our Country."

Trump's rhetoric also employs the *immigration as dangerous waters* metaphor, as when he tweets about "Criminal elements and DRUGS *pouring in*" and talks about stopping "this large *flow* of people, INCLUDING MANY CRIMINALS, from entering Mexico to U.S."[8] If immigrants are dangerous waters that "flow" or "pour" into a country, then the conceptual metaphor that describes the country is *nation as container*. In their work on foreign policy metaphors, Paul Chilton and George

Lakoff[9] note that "with the emergence of the modern nation-state," this metaphor has become "so well rooted in the mind that it is difficult to think of the present state-in-a-container system as anything other than a natural and immutable fact." This is evident not just in Trump's tweets but also in much reportage that reinforces the idea of "closing" or "sealing" the border as one would a container.

The container metaphor holds important implications for ideas about security. "Security for a state is conceptualized in terms of being inside an overwhelmingly strong container that stops things from getting in or out," Chilton and Lakoff write. When it is applied to immigration, the logical consequence is for the demagogue to peddle a border wall—a barrier to prevent "leaks" into the container. At the same time, the demagogue must stoke fear and anxiety by exaggerating the danger posed by immigrants entering the nation-as-container. As Trump tweets, "Building a great Border Wall, with drugs (poison) and enemy combatants *pouring* into our Country, is all about National Defense. Build WALL through M[ilitary]!" Notice how the dangerous waters metaphor is frequently collocated with the stereotypical trope of immigrants as criminals. Trump's frequent allusion to drugs plays on popular imagery of drug cartels and encourages an association between that imagery and immigrants.

But the predominant metaphor in Trump's tweets in the final weeks before the 2018 midterm elections was the military metaphor. Trump portrays *immigration as war,* variously referring to the migrant caravan as an "onslaught," "invasion," or "assault" on the nation. Immigrants themselves are correspondingly seen as a military force (*immigrants as soldiers*) and the nation-as-container concept takes on a militarized dimension (*nation as fortress*). Trump tweets about the country being "overrun by illegal immigrants" as a military stronghold might be overrun by an invading army.

The problem with the military metaphor is that—in demagogic fashion—it stokes fears of immigrants by falsely equating them with armed soldiers seeking to violently threaten a nation's sovereignty. Archetypical images of Nazi Germany's aggressive invasions of neighboring countries during World War II come to mind. But immigration is no more a war than it is a flood or disease. These metaphors stoke fear precisely because they draw vivid images from a source domain (e.g., war, flood, disease) while ignoring the incongruencies between the metaphorical model and the phenomenon being described (immigration).

Moreover, the military metaphor positions immigrants not just as invading soldiers engaged in a type of military conquest, but as dehumanized "enemies" worthy of fear and loathing. This contributes to the stark division between "us" and "them," eliding the common humanity between us. It turns families desperate to escape violence and poverty into "enemy combatants," as seen in Trump's tweet above.

The demagogue's vision of immigration is a far cry from the imagery of the immigrant-as-pilgrim celebrated every

Thanksgiving across the United States. It's a far cry from the "Give me your tired, your poor, your huddled masses yearning to breathe free" view of the United States as a nation of immigrants. Trump's immigration metaphors replace the positive descriptors of immigrants as beacons of hope, sources of new ideas, sowers of innovation, and harbingers of the cultural richness of American life.

When the demagogue takes his metaphors literally, we end up with a decision to "deploy at least 5,200 active-duty troops to the southern border"[10] to counter a so-called invasion of families looking for a better life. In his fearmongering tweets, Trump inveighs, "I am bringing out the military for this National Emergency. They will be stopped!" After all, according to the metaphors he lives by, "this is an invasion of our Country and our Military is waiting for you!"

As Norman Fairclough points out, "Different metaphors imply different ways of dealing with things."[11] Trump's metaphors lead to a show of force (emphasis on "show" since it elevates spectacle over genuine solutions like appointing more immigration judges) to placate the anxious voters he has riled up, much like Don Quixote tilting at windmills. Immigration metaphors like these are part of the broader conspiracy-oriented disinformation that has moved from the alt-right fringes to the mainstream through presidential amplification. It's no surprise that Trump's demagogic language can be seen in the social media posts of those who would take this hatred to violent extremes. The man who entered a Pittsburgh synagogue in

October 2018 and took the lives of 11 people also spoke of an "infestation" in US society and saw those in the migrant caravan as "invaders." In a post linking his anti-Semitism and xenophobia, the man impugned a Jewish organization dedicated to helping immigrants and refugees: "HIAS likes to bring *invaders* in that kill our people. I can't sit by and watch my people get slaughtered. Screw your optics, I'm going in."[12]

Despite what Trump's enablers pretend, the words uttered by the US president matter. His immigration metaphors do not constitute "plain speaking," "strong language," or "passionate debate," nor can they be innocently excused as his "own style," as Vice President Pence has contended.[13] His language is textbook demagoguery, and his immigration metaphors help constitute our current sociopolitical moment. To move beyond this moment requires more US voters to recognize and acknowledge these cheap, invidious demagogic appeals for what they are and support candidates who speak out against this politics of hate.

Post-truth was the *Oxford English Dictionary*'s word of the year in 2016, but the word became even more relevant in 2017 as Americans suffered through the first year of a presidency frighteningly indifferent, if not openly hostile, to facts. When it comes to exaggerations, half-truths, and outright fabrications, the Trump presidency is without precedent. According to the *Washington Post*, Trump "made 1,628 false or misleading claims over [his first] 298 days."[14] In a more conservative tally that omitted "any statement that could be plausibly defended" and "modest quantitative errors," the *New York Times* found that Trump "told 103 separate untruths, many of them repeatedly," in his first ten months in office.[15] Obama told 18 over the entirety of his two terms. "That's an average of about two a year for Obama and about 124 a year for Trump."[16]

Beyond the sheer quantity, Trump's incessant lying is also qualitatively different from his predecessors. Previous presidents would correct their statements when met with contrary evidence, the *New York Times* points out. But "Trump is different. When he is caught lying, he will often try to discredit people telling the truth." According to psychologist Bella DePaulo, Trump tells more self-serving lies and more cruel lies (i.e., "told to hurt or disparage others") than participants in her two decades of research on lying.[17]

But Trump's lies are not only self-serving. The lies serve to prop up the problematic worldview he peddles to his base. I found a striking pattern in the 103 statements compiled by the *New York Times*. Trump's lies engage in a practice that I will call the *typification of a worldview*. That is, his lies often depict a characteristic or representative picture of reality as viewed through the ideological lens of Trumpian conservatism. Factual fidelity is superseded by ideological fidelity to one or more axioms that undergird the system of beliefs of Trumpism. These include the tenets that immigrants are criminals, Muslims are terrorists, and voter fraud is rampant, among other claims that reinforce invidious stereotypes and erode trust in democratic institutions.

Take for example this statement, in which Trump takes credit for a decline in border crossings that began before he was sworn in as president: "Since I took office we have cut illegal immigration on our southern border by record numbers. 78 percent."[18] Or this statement, in which he claims that then president Enrique Peña Nieto of Mexico called him to relay the following message: "And even the President of Mexico called me—they said their southern border, very few people are coming because they know they're not going to get through our border, which is the ultimate compliment."[19] (Peña Nieto denied that any such call took place.) In both statements, although the lies are self-serving in that they allow Trump to flatter himself or take credit for something that isn't true, they also do important political work by reifying the Trumpian tenet that immigration poses a threat only his presidency can guard against.

Another tenet of the Trumpian worldview is a fear of foreigners and the equating of Muslims with terrorists. Here Trump paints this picture of the world through a false statement about the vetting of refugees: "We've taken in tens of thousands of people. We know nothing about them. They can say they vet them. They didn't vet them. They have no papers. How can you vet somebody when you don't know anything about them and you have no papers? How do you vet them? You can't." In fact, the vetting process at the time was quite rigorous and took up to two years. But the falsehood neatly captures the pillar of Trumpism that equates Muslim refugees with terrorists and stokes xenophobia.

The Trumpian worldview also views voter fraud as rampant. Despite a lack of evidence, Trump asserts that "between 3 million and 5 million illegal votes caused me to lose the popular vote."[20] The lie is not only narcissistically self-serving, but it also supports a worldview that elevates the nonissue of voter fraud to justify policies that disenfranchise legal voters.

Trump's lying does valuable political work. The lies build a compelling narrative of "the way things are," reinforcing a picture of reality that accords with what Trumpian conservatives already know and accept as true regardless of what the facts say. In other words, Trump's lies confirm a set of beliefs by promulgating "alternative facts" that remain ideologically faithful even if they lack factual verifiability. In many ways, a narrative based on misleading claims and fabricated evidence provides a more poignant and convincing depiction of reality than one based on banal facts—at least for those who share the worldview. What matters most for narrative believability, as Jerome Bruner points out, is verisimilitude rather than "empirical verification and logical requiredness."[21]

Trump's lying also does psychological work. The lies help maintain an intact mental model of that worldview when countervailing facts and evidence would otherwise lead to cognitive dissonance. As cognitive science research suggests, we are more likely to accept facts that accord with what we already believe and discount facts that do not. Moreover, providing empirical evidence to debunk false claims—like political fact-checking sites do—can backfire when that evidence threatens a worldview.[22] Trump's blatant lies and the fact-checking of those lies may have little effect on his most die-hard supporters, who view the Trumpian worldview as commonsense, or simply as the way things are.

For the rest of us, Trump's incessant lying has led more people to override our "truth bias," the bias we have toward assuming others are telling the truth.[23] "We no longer give Trump the benefit of the doubt that we usually give so readily."[24] That may be a necessary survival strategy, but the erosion of trust among the public and lack of factual integrity in the White House create substantial problems for democracy.

3 POLITICAL THEATER AND SPECTACLE

Stagecraft has long been part of American politics, from slick campaign ads to carefully choreographed acceptance speeches at nationally televised conventions. But with Trump, political stagecraft has moved into the realm of self-obsessed spectacle more akin to reality television than politics per se. On the campaign trail and in the White House, Trump has put on a show that has flaunted the rules of what it means to be politically viable. Whereas most politicians strive to maintain a consistent political image, Trump revels in inconsistency, sometimes contradicting himself within a single sitting. Trump's primary concerns seem to be with his ego and putting on a show with little regard for the actual job of governing.

The essays in this section try to make sense of the spectacle of Trumpian politics. Why would voters rank Trump higher than Clinton on honesty prior to the 2016 election despite the overwhelming number of outlandish claims and outright fabrications he told? How does Trump create a coherent political image despite his fickleness as a politician? How do we explain the flouting of norms that marks the Trump presidency? Here we pay close attention to the interpretive frames that journalists, politicians, and voters use to vet candidates and hold them politically accountable for their words and actions.

WHEN THE DISCOURSE
OF THEATER TRUMPS TRUTH

Of the many disturbing trends surrounding Trump's ascendancy to the White House, the slipperiness of his words most perplexes many intellectuals and political reporters. Unlike most politicians, Trump never seems to be held fully accountable for the words he utters. His statements, no matter how outlandish, fail to stick to him the same way that, say, President George H. W. Bush's "read my lips" pledge on taxes did.[1]

To understand why, it's helpful to turn to Jane Hill's analysis of the elder Bush's infamous pledge on taxes at the 1988 Republican National Convention. In "'Read My Article': Ideological Complexity and the Over-Determination of Promising in American Presidential Politics," Hill distinguishes between two discourses that underpin American politics: the *discourse of truth* and the *discourse of theater*.[2] Both are ever present, even as one or the other comes to the fore at any given moment.

Everyone is familiar with the discourse of truth since much political discussion operates through this frame. This is the discourse that places a premium on fact-checking. It focuses on issues of truth, lies, and promises. When operating within this discourse, we assume that what a politician says corresponds (or not) to some state of affairs in the world that can be objectively verified. Philosophers call this the correspondence theory of truth. If a politician's words match the world, then the facts can be said to check out. If the words do not correspond, then the politician can be branded a liar.

As Hill describes, this discourse of truth relies on what linguists call the referential function of language. The referential function values language primarily as a way to communicate information, as a vehicle for imparting knowledge. But language has many more functions than just its referential, or denotational function.[3] Language also has poetic, emotive, conative, phatic, and metalingual functions. For example, we draw on the phatic function of language when talking to a baby. The words we utter allow us to connect on a human-to-human level. In such an encounter, the referential function is mostly irrelevant; we may not be trying to convey any information at all. Likewise, when we exclaim loudly after stubbing a toe, the referential function takes a backseat to the emotive function.

In 1988, George H. W. Bush stood before a convention of cheering Republicans and uttered six words that came back to haunt him later in his presidency: "Read my lips. No new taxes." Interpreting these words through the discourse of truth, as many Americans did, involved taking the words as a promise—an expectation that referential continuity would be maintained between his stated intention at that moment and future actions he would take as president. However, that referential continuity evaporated when Bush signed a bill in 1990 that included some tax increases. The supposed promise became a broken promise, and its implications for his character (e.g., not being "a man of his word") undermined his reelection bid.

But there is another discourse that also underlies politics: the discourse of theater. Instead of the referential function of language, the discourse of theater shifts the focus to the poetic function of language. Central to the discourse of theater is "message" in the sense of, as Hill describes, "a set of themes deployed through performance." Message may involve words, but the words are used to convey emotion and speak to a politician's general ideological orientation rather than specific policy details. Viewing Bush's convention speech through the discourse of theater is to see it as a dramatic enactment of the shared Republican disdain for taxes. The point was to rally supporters and emphasize the philosophical perspective he would carry into future negotiations with Congress.

As Hill describes, "To generate a favorable emotional tone in voters, message must play to their desires." Trump excels at crafting a message that plays to voters' desires. In his own performance stagecraft, he uses "entertainment, gesture, and spectacle"[4] to create a spectacular show for audiences. For his supporters, the referential dimension of his words seems to matter less than the emotional message they convey. He speaks—and tweets—not to lay out policy details, but to rally supporters and convey a general populist attitude toward the establishment.

Although the discourses of truth and theater have both always been part of US politics, the rise of Trump illustrates what happens when the two are disproportionately applied to presidential candidates. On the one hand, Trump's outlandish and often contradictory statements seem to have been mostly interpreted through the discourse of theater by many of his voters. As a former reality-TV star, Trump comports himself like a celebrity rather than a politician. This helps frame his discourse as spectacle, which seems to immunize him from the flip-flopper label even in the absence of consistent statements on the campaign trail.

On the other hand, mainstream political reportage relies on the discourse of truth to vet candidates for public office, discern their policy positions, and hold them accountable. While candidate Trump's fabrications were given a pass by a large portion of the electorate, the same cannot be said for Hillary Clinton, whose statements were primarily viewed through the discourse of truth by voters. This unbalanced application of interpretive frames—viewing Trump primarily through the discourse of theater and Clinton primarily through the discourse of truth—may partially explain the staggering results of preelection polls that ranked Trump higher than Clinton on honesty.[5] This occurred despite fact-checking sites like PolitiFact having documented Trump's statements as 70 percent untruthful versus the mirror opposite for Clinton.[6]

It is possible that Trump's supporters will eventually turn to the discourse of truth when the message he sold on the campaign trail fails to come to fruition, much like George H. W. Bush's supporters did. But there is little sign of that happening even as his legal and ethical troubles continue to mount. In this new world of "alternative facts" and demagoguery, Trump simply blames others for any promises he fails to keep. No matter how outlandish the excuses, this move seems to keep his most ardent supporters by his side.

The real question, though, will be how journalists and voters use these frames to vet candidates in the next presidential election. Will there be a more balanced approach with Trump running as an incumbent politician, or will he continue to be held to a different standard than his challengers when it comes to truth and factual accountability?

TRUMP FIRST AND THE PRESENTATION
OF THE POLITICAL SELF

Politicians typically strive to project a stable political persona free of self-contradictions and inconsistencies. President Trump, on the other hand, is full of self-contradictions and inconsistencies. But underlying this apparently incoherent political self is a different type of coherence—one that maintains an egotistical self-image rather than stable political positions.[7]

Trump's political fickleness took center stage in a White House meeting to discuss immigration legislation with bipartisan members of the Senate in January 2018. In that meeting, with cameras rolling, he called for a "bill of love" and declared that "he was willing to 'take the heat' politically" for a bipartisan compromise.[8] Senator Diane Feinstein asked Trump, "What about a clean DACA [Deferred Action for Childhood Arrivals] bill now with the commitment that we go into a comprehensive immigration reform procedure?" Trump responded, "I have no problem with that." Feinstein followed up to confirm, "Would you be agreeable to that?" "Yeah, I would like that," said Trump.[9]

After Representative Kevin McCarthy voiced objections, Trump contradicted his moments-earlier stance in support of a clean DACA bill. The exchange illustrated the confusing tenor of the meeting in which Trump made contradictory statements about where he stood and insisted that he would sign whatever legislation Congress sent him: "I'm signing it." Only a few days later in another meeting with senators, Trump followed his call for a "bill of love" with a call for racially motivated exclusion. In that closed-door meeting, Trump left Senators Durbin and Graham "stunned" with his racist attitudes toward immigration.[10] Then, in the weeks that followed, his claim to sign anything legislators came up with shifted to a refusal to sign anything without money for a border wall. The immigration debate is not the first time lawmakers on both sides of the aisle have found Trump to be an "untrustworthy, chronically inconsistent" negotiator.[11] This inconsistency is par for the course with the Trump presidency.

Trump's apparent inconsistency appears at odds with the way politicians, as Alessandro Duranti describes, typically "worry about how to project and maintain an image of themselves as beings whose past, present, and future actions, beliefs, and evaluations follow some clear basic principles, none of which contradicts another."[12] That is, they strive to maintain *existential coherence* and avoid accusations of flip-flopping.[13] As Duranti shows in his analysis of Walter Capps's mid-1990s congressional campaign, a typical politician strives to construct a coherent political self through consistent words and actions.

Trump's rampant inconsistency on policy issues, not to mention the way his words and tweets exhibit factual inconsistencies, provides a stark contrast to Duranti's case study of Walter Capps. But Trump does exhibit a type of existential coherence. It's just that it has little to do with traditional political concerns. Trump's existential coherence revolves around his personal image rather than his political self. Trump strives to promote his own personal brand, which centers on a self-conception of being the smartest guy in the room. Trump's most consistent message is his egocentric projection of a self-made man endowed with natural talent and superior intelligence. As Trump has tweeted, "my two greatest assets have been mental stability and being, like, really smart." He continued, "I went from VERY successful businessman, to top T.V. Star . . . to President of the United States (on my first try). I think that would qualify as not smart, but genius . . . and a very stable genius at that!"

A better term for Trump's existential coherence is *egocentric coherence* since his words and actions point to an excessive preoccupation with self-image. This egocentric coherence eclipses the normal drive among politicians to achieve political coherence or even factual consistency. This can be seen from the first days of his presidency when Trump insisted the crowd size at his inauguration broke records. It continues with his refusal to acknowledge Russian interference in the 2016 election because that would "call into question the idea that he won the election on his own merits."[14]

To maintain this egocentric coherence, Trump consistently engages in *self-serving bias*—attributing success to personal qualities and efforts, while blaming external factors for failure. When the stock market rises, Trump credits his election and claims "it is because of me."[15] When it drops, he blames it on others. These dual faces of the self-serving bias epitomize Trump's presidency.

In the face of threats to his egocentric coherence, Trump readily engages in the blame game—a move that stems from the way self-threat increases the self-serving bias.[16] When a judge halted his travel ban, Trump preemptively blamed the judge for any future terrorist attack. When his administration encountered difficulty with an intransigent North Korea, Trump blamed China for not curbing the nation's nuclear program. He blamed Congress for poor US relations with Russia; McConnell and Ryan for a debt-ceiling "mess"; and Democrats for DACA failures.

The only time Trump seems to care about political consistency is when an apparent lack of it threatens his egocentric coherence. This may explain why Trump took umbrage when his chief of staff, John Kelly, told reporters in January 2018 that Trump's promise to build a wall had not been "fully informed" and that his position had "evolved."[17] Trump could have easily acknowledged that his position "evolved" and maintained political coherence by pointing to "a higher-order logic that justifies the change," a general strategy often invoked by politicians, as Duranti explains.[18] But Trump instead shot back to protect his ego and maintain the self-image of a person endowed with superior intelligence. Maintaining this egocentric coherence upstaged political calculations to arrive at an immigration bill.

Trump projects a different form of existential coherence than the "coherence of actions, thoughts, and words" that politicians typically pursue.[19] Trump's egocentric coherence exhibits all the signs of narcissism and is enabled by the sycophants surrounding him. Needless to say, this is no way to govern a democracy.

Nothing better epitomizes the content-free showmanship of President Trump's governing style than the White House Rose Garden ceremony he held in May 2017 after the House passed its version of a bill to repeal the Affordable Care Act. Never mind that such a ceremony is "typically reserved for legislation that is being signed into law, not for a controversial bill that passed just one chamber,"[20] or that weeks later he called the legislation "mean."[21] And then there were his "confusing, and in some cases, outright incorrect"[22] remarks to Senate Republicans on healthcare as he implored senators to pass something—anything—so that they could "all go over to the Oval Office" and hold another signing ceremony to celebrate.[23] The content of the legislation and the details of the policies mattered less than the made-for-television spectacle of Trump's performance.[24]

We have entered a political era where policy matters less than spectacle. No doubt, as both candidate and now president, Trump has exhibited a "flagrant indifference to the details of public policy."[25] Trump's appeal on the campaign trail instead arose, as Kira Hall, Donna Goldstein, and Matthew Ingram show, from his carnivalesque comedic performances that simultaneously empowered supporters and horrified critics—compelling supporters and critics alike to behold the spectacle.[26]

Mikhail Bakhtin's concept of the carnivalesque—a mocking or satirical challenge to traditional authority—provides insight into Trump's ability to subvert dominant political conventions through humor and chaos, maximizing entertainment value as he flouts presidential norms.[27] But this concept alone cannot do full justice to explaining the ongoing, day-to-day spectacle of Trump's presidency. To better understand the Trump phenomenon, we need to borrow a concept from the world of professional wrestling, where hyperreality converges with spectacle to produce the same strange amalgamation of bravado, hyperbole, and exaggeration (and outright lies) that marks Trumpian politics. That concept is *kayfabe.*

Originating with carnival workers, the term *kayfabe* passed into the world of wrestling "to mean the illusion of realness"[28] or "wrestlers' adherence to the big lie, the insistence that the unreal is real."[29] Kayfabe involves a "willing suspension of disbelief that allows fans to buy into often fictionalized story lines, larger-than-life personalities and match results."[30] In other words, as sociologist Nick Rogers explains, kayfabe is "the unspoken contract between wrestlers and spectators."[31] That contract goes like this: "We'll present you something clearly fake under the insistence that it's real, and you will experience genuine emotion. Neither party acknowledges the bargain, or else the magic is ruined."

Kayfabe ensures that Trumpian political discourse is largely read through the discourse of theater as opposed to the discourse of truth, since the discourse of theater provides a lens for viewing political statements as a type of performance art. Truth and accuracy become less important than the entertainment value of words, gestures, and tweets and the emotional tone and ideological stance they carry.

But kayfabe is more than just an interpretive framework that privileges the discourse of theater over the discourse of truth. Kayfabe allows Trumpian discourse to create its own internal reality filled with "alternative facts" that are used to determine what is true. In other words, kayfabe ensures that questions of truth and accuracy are not judged according to standards established outside the fourth wall of the theater, but inside the story world constructed on the stage or in the wrestling ring—or on the reality-television set of the Trump White House.

Like the drama of professional wrestling, Trumpian politics consists of continually advancing a compelling story line. The precise content of that story line matters less than the spectacle it creates. Wrestling characters include "faces" (good guys) and "heels" (bad guys). Matches involve "angles" (scripted feuds) between the characters, and the unfolding story line contains a number of "swerves" (shocking turns) to elicit "heat" (crowd reactions, especially negative ones). Success in the ring is measured by the amount of heat generated, and drawn-out matches are filled with what Roland Barthes called a "spectacle of excess."[32]

William Stodden and John Hansen claim that we have "a population which is largely conditioned to see heroes and villains in politics the same way they see heroes and villains in professional wrestling." Trumpian politics certainly feeds off and plays into that conditioning. Whether one sees Trump as a "face" or "heel" depends on one's political perspective. But even heels can be crowd favorites: "These were characters that most fans loved to hate but that many fans also idolized because they represented the breaking of norms with impunity."[33]

Trumpian politics is filled with wrestling's larger-than-life characters, angles, and swerves that generate (mostly negative) heat as Trump breaks norms with impunity. Trump's feuds take place within his own party and even within his own administration, not just across party lines. Trump versus James Comey, the FBI director he fired in an apparent effort to obstruct justice. Trump versus Jeff Sessions, the "beleaguered" attorney general that he himself appointed before embarking on a cyberbullying campaign against him. Trump versus Robert Mueller, the reputable special counsel in charge of the now-complete Russia investigation. And of course, Trump versus his always ready-to-resurrect foil, Hillary "Lock her up!" Clinton. Trump gets help from tag-team partners like Anthony Scaramucci, the short-lived White House communications director who joined "The Donald" with his own ready-made stage name ("The Mooch") and a complementary no-holds-barred demeanor.

The next swerve, or shocking turn of events, may involve any number of angles; but certain tropes are frequently exploited to maximize the spectacle. In both wrestling entertainment and Trumpian politics, the angles inevitably involve nationalism, xenophobia, race, and class. "Since the early days of professional wrestling," Stodden and Hansen point out, "the 'foreign menace' has been a standard go-to tactic used by promoters to draw crowd interest." Beginning with "Hacksaw" Jim Duggan and Wrestle Mania IV, kayfabe has inspired crowds to respond to the "foreign menace" with chants of U-S-A. Trump campaign rallies do the same and add chants of "build the wall" as Trump incredulously tells the audience that Mexico will pay for it—or that maybe Congress will pay for it under threat of a government shutdown.

The lack of logic or verifiable content behind the showmanship does not matter. "Kayfabe isn't about factual verifiability," Rogers emphasizes; "it's about emotional fidelity." It's about creating a spectacle that validates the audience's feelings and provides a cathartic release. Trumpian politics may approximate the carnivalesque, but it closely mirrors the kayfabe of wrestling entertainment.

4   RESPONSIBILITY AND DENIABILITY

Language provides various ways for us to take ownership of words and actions or, conversely, to shirk responsibility for things we have previously said or done. Politicians are well known for playing language games that allow them to variously communicate or deny controversial claims. President Bill Clinton's defense during his impeachment hearings in 1998 depended upon (in his words) "what the meaning of the word 'is' is" when questioned about the veracity of his statement that "there's nothing going on between us" (referring to his relationship with Monica Lewinsky). President George W. Bush bolstered his case for an invasion of Iraq in 2003 by largely intimating that a strong connection existed between Saddam Hussein and Al-Qaeda (despite the lack of any evidence of direct ties). But language games like these have found a natural home in the Trump presidency amid a loose relationship with truth and a flair for spectacle.

The essays in this section explore how to hold politicians like Trump accountable for detestable statements and actions. What linguistic moves does Trump make to avoid responsibility for the veracity of false claims that he inserts into the national discourse? How does he engage in the language game of plausible deniability—for example, after mocking the physical disability of *New York Times* journalist Serge Kovaleski? Decoding these moves can help expose the absurd assumptions underlying a grifter's specious performances.

RESPONSIBILITY AND EVIDENCE
IN TRUMPIAN DISCOURSE

It started as an innocuous press conference in the White House Rose Garden with President Trump and Senate Majority Leader Mitch McConnell meeting with reporters to emphasize (despite all evidence to the contrary) that they were "closer than ever before."[1] Then Trump got a question about the deaths of four American soldiers who were killed in Niger on October 4, 2017.[2]

"And what do you have to say about that?" a reporter asked.

Trump replied that he had written letters to the families, which would be "going out tonight," and that he would "call the parents and the families—because I have done that, traditionally."

Never one to let a moment pass (even one of apolitical solemnity) without engaging in his favorite game of one-upmanship, he added that "if you look at President Obama and other presidents, most of them didn't make calls, a lot of them didn't make calls. I like to call when it's appropriate, when I think I'm able to do it."

Later in the press conference, a reporter followed up by asking how Trump could make that claim. Trump responded, "I was told that he didn't often." This exchange not only exemplifies Trump's constant need to puff himself up by denigrating others, but it also illustrates the way he exploits what linguists call *evidentiality*—the semantic marking of an information source—to wrap innuendos in the sheath of truth claims while avoiding responsibility for the veracity of those claims.

At the beginning of the 20th century, anthropologist Franz Boas observed in studying Native American languages that some languages require speakers to indicate an information source when speaking. For example, in Kwakiutl, Boas found four "suffixes denoting the source of information," whether by hearsay or other means.[3] Boas was particularly interested in the way languages like Kwakiutl encoded sources of information as obligatory grammatical elements,[4] something not done in European languages like English or French. Linguists since Boas have refined and elaborated the concept of evidentiality.

Linguists have debated whether the concept of evidentiality should solely refer to obligatory grammatical items that indicate an information source (like the verbal suffixes Boas found in Kwakiutl) or also extend to optional lexical expressions like the one Trump used to qualify his information source ("I was told"). Even though English lacks obligatory verbal elements to encode evidentiality, information sources can be encoded in discourse through the use of adverbs (e.g., *apparently*, *reportedly*) and other expressions (*it seems to me, it looks like, sounds like*).

Linguist Barbara Fox points out how verbs, adjectives, and adverbs function as evidential markers in conversational English, allowing speakers to choose evidential marking to distance themselves from claims or, conversely, employ "zero marking" (the absence of an evidential marker) to lay claim to greater authority or responsibility.[5] As an interesting case in point, Trump uses evidential markers to avoid taking personal responsibility for the veracity of claims, like his statement that "*I was told* that he [Obama] didn't often [call families of fallen service members]." Crucially, instances like this represent strategic usages for a man otherwise eager to assert authority and take responsibility for everything and anything that can be perceived as flattering to himself. How many times have we heard him take responsibility for creating millions of jobs since he took office—using a zero-evidential marker (in Fox's terminology).

In situations like the Rose Garden press conference Trump opts to use overt-evidential markers to slip in innuendos while distancing himself from the truth value of the claim. This works because evidentials merely supply the information source without indicating whether the statement attributed to the source is true or not. In other words, the truth value of a statement is unaffected by the evidential marker.

Take, for example, the way Trump fueled the "birther" movement. On August 6, 2012, Trump tweeted, "An 'extremely credible source' has called my office and told me that @BarackObama's birth certificate is a fraud." By including the evidential marker *X told me* to mark the claim that *Obama's birth certificate is a fraud*, Trump is able to act as a conduit for a lie without actually taking responsibility for the lie. The statement that *X told me* may be true even though the claim that *Obama's birth certificate is a fraud* is false. As linguist Alexandra Aikhenvald writes, "Linguistic evidentials can in fact be manipulated in rather intricate ways in telling lies."[6]

Trump is quite good at these types of manipulative linguistic moves, as a number of political journalists have noted. *New York Times* columnist Charles Blow points out that "Trump has found a way to couch the lies so that people believe they don't emanate from him but pass through him."[7] He does this through the strategic use of evidential markers and what Jenna Johnson of the *Washington Post* calls "Trump's they-said-it-not-me tactic."[8] Johnson explains how he "frequently couches his most controversial comments this way, which allows him to share a controversial idea, piece of tabloid gossip or conspiracy theory without technically embracing it. If the comment turns out to be popular, Trump will often drop the distancing qualifier—'people think' or 'some say.' If the opposite happens, Trump can claim that he never said the thing he is accused of saying."

Discursive moves that employ overt-evidential marking provide Trump with that all-important political cover known as *plausible deniability*, allowing him to peddle everything from fringe conspiracy theories to outright lies. A seasoned con artist couldn't play the game any better. But then again, *I was told* that Trump is a con artist. If that's true, and I'm not saying it is, it would mean he has really pulled the con of the century by becoming president.

We are accustomed to watching politicians play the language game of plausible deniability, but Donald Trump takes this game to a new level.[9] As Kira Hall and colleagues propose, Trump's gestural-rich "bodily displays, together with Trump's easy deniability of what he intended by them, suggests that comedic gesture may accomplish ideological work that exceeds even what can be conveyed in the already protected category of verbal humor."[10]

A prime illustration is the way Trump—with the help of surrogates—has refused to take full ownership of his mocking insult of *New York Times* reporter Serge Kovaleski on the campaign trail in November 2015. Commentators keep revisiting this particular incident—as Meryl Streep did in her speech at the Golden Globes on January 8, 2017—due to both its egregious nature and Trump's insistence that he was doing something different than what most saw him doing; namely, mocking a man's physical disability.

Trump responded to Meryl Streep with a series of tweets to convey his own preferred interpretation of the incident:

> Meryl Streep, one of the most over-rated actresses in Hollywood, doesn't know me but attacked last night at the Golden Globes. She is a . . .

Hillary flunky who lost big. For the 100th time, I never "mocked" a disabled reporter (would never do that) but simply showed him . . .

"groveling" when he totally changed a 16 year old story that he had written in order to make me look bad. Just more very dishonest media!

Plausible deniability is central to political discourse. What makes deniability oftentimes plausible is the ambiguity between what a speaker says in so many words and what a speaker intends to convey. A speaker can imply something without explicitly saying it, through the use of what philosopher H. P. Grice terms *implicature*.[11] For example, I can communicate a request to close the window by saying *It's cold in here*. If you are sitting near the window, you would get my meaning even though I didn't explicitly direct you to close the window. Contrary to a popular misconception about language, meaning is not fixed in words—an idea Michael Reddy addressed in his 1979 critique of the "conduit metaphor."[12] Meaning, as linguistic anthropologists emphasize, is an interactional accomplishment.

Plausible deniability thrives upon implicatures that are derivable only in a specific context (like the example of my request to close the window). As discourse is lifted out of one context and inserted into another, the ability to uncover a particular implicature from the previous context becomes harder to maintain and hence easier to deny. This is because the process of recontextualization opens up the discourse to the accrual of new meanings.

As Trump's remarks enter into new contexts, they point back to—or index—the originating context in which they were performed, in this case on November 21, 2015. The reported speech thereby carries meanings established in that context. But those meanings can be creatively reworked just as easily as they can be faithfully recreated. That is, social meanings can be variously affirmed and reimagined in line with the demands of the current interactional context.

To understand the consensus interpretation of Trump's remarks, Grice's maxim of relation helps. This maxim demands that communicators "be relevant." In Trump's embodied performance of Kovaleski, viewers need to find some sort of relevance between Trump's body language and his accompanying words. In his performance, Trump voices Kovaleski, saying, "I don't know what I said. . . . I don't remember." Simultaneously, he flails his arms and contracts his wrists. The words convey an air of incompetence, especially as ventriloquized through Trump's mocking tone. But his bodily gestures seem to have little to do with incompetence per se. What is the implicature here?

For viewers familiar with images of Kovaleski, Trump's gestures can be seen to embody his physical mannerisms. Kovaleski has a congenital condition known as arthrogryposis, a disability that causes joint contractures in his right arm and wrist. But even for viewers unfamiliar with Kovaleski's physical condition, some sort of relevance must be drawn between the verbal message of incompetence and contracting wrists; those viewers might default to a generic image of a person with a developmental disability, where a physical disability metonymically stands in for an intellectual disability. This would allow viewers—even those unfamiliar with Kovaleski—to get the "joke" in which Trump mocks Kovaleski's intellectual competence.

To explain in terms of indexicality, Trump's bodily gestures either directly index Kovaleski's arthrogryposis (for those familiar with Kovaleski) or indirectly index Kovaleski's supposed incompetence by associating his intellectual ability with an unspecified developmental disability. In either case, it's difficult to sidestep the interpretation that this performance uses Kovaleski's physical condition to mock and insult him—much like a playground bully might do.

Given this consensus interpretation, how does Trump find wiggle room to claim plausible deniability? He reframes the unspoken social meaning associated with his gestures by questioning the relevance others find between those gestures and his words. Whereas the consensus interpretation draws from the indexical association between Trump's gestures and a physical disability—namely, Kovaleski's arthrogryposis—Trump imposes a different indexical association on his recontextualized performance, associating his gestures instead with the movements made by someone engaged in an act of groveling.

Although groveling typically involves prostrating oneself on the ground and moving about in an obsequious manner—quite different from Trump's performance of uncontrolled joint contractures—the ambiguity of bodily gestures allows Trump to cast enough doubt to challenge the obvious interpretation. And this is how the entertainer-in-chief takes this language game to an unprecedented level in presidential politics. He revels at playing with the media in difficult-to-defend cases like this that would sink most politicians.

Whether the plausible deniability actually convinces anyone or not is beside the point. Playing this plausible deniability game allows Trump to reinforce an overriding message of his populism: the supposed obsession "liberal elites" have with enforcing "political correctness." *Look at Meryl Streep!* he says. *Look at the dopey professor writing this essay! Liberal intellectuals can't take a joke.* And his supporters chortle in agreement.

The question remains how to effectively counter Trump in his (largely Twitter-based) language games. Perhaps it starts by exposing the absurd assumptions required to play these games with a straight face. Then we can see them more clearly as games of distraction or, as linguist George Lakoff explains,[13] diversion tweets; and thereby, as *New York Times* columnist David Brooks suggests, stop treating them "as if they are arguments."[14]

5 THE PROPAGATION OF CONSPIRACY THEORIES

Propaganda carries decidedly negative connotations in contemporary English, denoting biased or misleading information. Central to this meaning is a focus on the widespread dissemination of this information, which is captured in the etymology of the word from the Latin verb *propagare* meaning "to spread or to propagate."

Originally, propaganda applied to the dissemination of religious doctrine and carried positive connotations. The term entered the domain of politics around World War I when it was applied to the propagation of information in support of a political cause. But as the 20th century advanced, propaganda came to be largely associated with the propagation of intentionally misleading information. Now, in the 21st century, technology and the power of the Trump presidency combine to propagate various forms of misinformation, from wild conspiracy theories to inaccurate claims that take on a life of their own once they enter into public discourse.

The essays in this section deconstruct how the power of the presidency helps Trump spread false claims, give power to conspiracy theories, and engage in what historian Richard Hofstadter characterized in 1964 as the "paranoid style of politics." Gaining critical awareness of the processes underlying the spread of misinformation can help to more effectively guard against it.

PLAYING TELEPHONE WITH THE POWER OF THE PRESIDENCY

Ordinarily, groundless conspiratorial accusations forwarded by political pundits—like the false claim that President Obama wiretapped Donald Trump's phone during the 2016 presidential campaign—do not receive serious recognition from the US Congress, let alone promises from the chair of the House Intelligence Committee to investigate those accusations.[1]

However, President Trump's tweet on March 4, 2017, that "Obama had my 'wires tapped' in Trump Tower" is a reminder that these are not ordinary times. Trump followed his first tweet with several more—none of which provided any evidence to substantiate the accusation. Yet the claim continued to propagate. It moved from conservative media to the voice of the president, on to the president's press secretary, and then to Representative Devin Nunes who said the House Intelligence Committee, which he led at the time, would investigate.

This shrewd political move in Machiavellian terms (if only it had been strategically planned) immediately shifted the mainstream media's focus from revelations about Attorney General Jeff Sessions's meetings with the Russian ambassador during the campaign (despite his previous claim he never met with any Russians), and sent political reporters and Congress on a wild-goose chase. In ordinary times, a wild-goose chase might have been avoided; but not during these times, as the president of the United States continues to brand investigative journalism "fake news" and makes Fox News his go-to source for facts—or rather, "alternative facts." The result is the exploitation of the symbolic power of the presidency to elevate suspect claims to the level of serious debate.

How does the discursive power of the presidency operate to elevate an evidence-free claim like this? The answer lies in the way symbolic power intersects with intertextual speech chains.

In *Language and Symbolic Power*, Pierre Bourdieu makes the point that "authority comes to language from outside, a fact concretely exemplified by the *skeptron* that, in Homer, is passed to the orator who is about to speak."[2] As Bourdieu conveys with this imagery, the power of words to shape sociopolitical reality comes from "the *delegated power of* the spokesperson"—that is, the power vested in the office of the spokesperson.

Before taking the oath of office, Trump's outlandish tweets and claims—such as those that fueled the "birther" movement—may have gained a following, but certainly were not elevated to the level of congressional inquiry. But as president, he now holds the equivalent of the Homerian skeptron. The symbolic power of the office imbues his words with greater force and authority. The power of the presidency allows Trump to authenticate claims circulated by conservative radio hosts and websites. Those claims enter into an intertextual speech chain as they are passed from one person to the next. Typically, this kind of intertextual speech chain would stay on the political fringe, but the claims now gain momentum through the delegated power of President Trump as their spokesperson.

The claims made by radio pundit Mark Levin and passed along to Breitbart News and then to Donald Trump form a special type of intertextual speech chain that Judith Irvine calls a *chain of authentication*. In her 1989 article "When Talk Isn't Cheap: Language and Political Economy," Irvine draws from philosopher Hilary Putnam to coin this term.[3] In his 1975 essay "The Meaning of Meaning," Putnam explains that for most of us to determine the value of a material item such as a gold ring, we rely "on a special subclass of speakers" to authenticate that item.[4] Think, for example, of experienced jewelers whose expertise in precious metals allows them to differentiate between items that simply look like gold and "whether or not something is really gold." As Irvine explains, "These people are experts whose knowledge . . . renders their usage of the term *gold* authoritative. The economic and symbolic value of gold for the wider community depends on this." But we rarely rely on "a single testimonial statement." Rather, we rely on "a *chain of authentication*, a historical sequence by which an expert's attestation . . . is relayed to other people."[5] Irvine notes that this process applies to "not only material objects, but also verbal items like magic spells or other texts."

As I describe elsewhere, these verbal items include truth claims put forth by politicians.[6] Take, for example, the claims forwarded by President George W. Bush and his administration about supposed links between Saddam Hussein and Osama bin Laden. The claims relied on a chain of authentication that stretched from various administration officials—Vice President Dick Cheney, National Security Advisor Condoleezza Rice, and Secretary of State Colin Powell—to foreign leaders. Along the way, the symbolic power of the speakers involved in the intertextual speech chain worked to authenticate the claims as authoritative versions of the geopolitical situation, despite widespread evidence to the contrary.

In the same way, the symbolic power of the presidency wielded by Trump works to authenticate fringe conspiracy theories offered up by factually unreliable websites. His voice acts as a valuable linchpin in the chain of authentication to give those ideas some semblance of credibility to the wider public (as evidenced by the seriousness with which the public and Congress treated the tweets).

But unlike the regimented messaging operation carried out by the Bush administration to drum up support for the invasion of Iraq, Trump's tweets are anything but highly organized and controlled. The message put forth by the Bush administration about Saddam Hussein and terrorism generally remained faithful from one speaker to another as it propagated through the intertextual speech chain. However, remarks originating with conservative pundits and culminating with Trump's tweets lack fidelity across the different contexts in which they have been reiterated.

In the case of Trump, the intertextual connections work more like a game of telephone where the message input at the beginning of the speech chain transmogrifies by the time it reaches Trump's Twitter feed. Along the way, unsubstantiated rants become serious claims worthy of congressional inquiry. But while the political establishment treats the tweets as falsifiable allegations, the claims-in-search-of-evidence act as evidence in their own right for those who already share the general ideological message they emote (via the discourse of theater). After all, as White House officials have suggested (by invoking plausible deniability), Trump's claim "was not meant to be taken literally,"[7] except, on White House insistence, where it was meant to be taken as a call for Congress to investigate "the fact that President Obama was tapping my phones."

The Trump administration's embrace of anti-intellectualism is fueled by conspiracy theories that call scientific evidence into question. A case in point is the response of administration officials to the unprecedented hurricane season in 2017.[8]

After the flooding in Houston due to Hurricane Harvey, Michael Mann, a leading scientific voice on climate change, detailed the ways that climate change worsened the impact of the storm.[9] Hurricane Harvey and, soon after, Hurricanes Irma and Maria provided real-life case studies of the dire consequences predicted by climate change models: as ocean temperatures increase due to global warming, hurricanes are likely to be more severe and bring more rainfall.

But in the wake of the devastation left by Hurricane Irma in Florida, EPA administrator Scott Pruitt told CNN that it would be "very, very insensitive" to have a discussion about climate change, deflecting attempts to consider its real-world impacts.[10] Pruitt, of course, was the ideal EPA administrator for a president who, echoing Republican senator James Inhofe, has consistently referred to climate change as a "hoax" and pulled the United States out of the Paris climate accord.

Through its actions and appointments, the Trump administration has elevated climate change denial to official government policy. The administration's position represents a fundamental shift away from science toward the embrace of what Richard Hofstadter in 1964 termed the "paranoid style in American politics." Rife with "qualities of heated exaggeration, suspiciousness, and conspiratorial fantasy," the paranoid style excels at spinning alternative narratives to explain away the scientific consensus on climate change.[11]

Making an analogy with the clinical paranoiac (while avoiding a psychiatric diagnosis), Hofstadter points out how the spokesperson of the paranoid style sees a "hostile and conspiratorial world" that is "directed against a nation, a culture, a way of life." For those who practice the paranoid style, "a vast and sinister conspiracy" exists all around them, perpetuated by a well-organized and wily enemy that engages in secret schemes and behind-the-scene plots. The enemy employs a "gigantic and yet subtle machinery of influence set in motion to undermine and destroy a way of life." Distinct from simply acknowledging an occasional conspiratorial act in history (think Watergate, a coup d'état, or an assassination plot), the spokesperson of the paranoid style views conspiracy "as *the motive force* in historical events."[12]

For example, in his book *The Greatest Hoax*, Senator Inhofe turns his worst conspiratorial fears into an explanation for why climate change has been elevated as a serious issue by what he calls "alarmists." He claims that "the entire global warming, climate-change issue" is "an effort to dramatically and hugely increase regulation" and "to raise our cost of living and taxes."[13] Inhofe turns his concerns about the potential impacts of climate change policies (such as more regulations and higher taxes) into the underlying motivation of those involved with the issue. Many climate change denial narratives apply this type of conspiratorial logic to claim that scientists and environmentalists have manufactured the threat of climate change for self-serving interests. The "pervasiveness of conspiracy theories in the debate about human-induced climate change" has a long track record; there is an "ease with which unverified claims and suggestions of conspiracy are disseminated among sympathetic audiences," writes anthropologist Myanna Lahsen in her work on climate change communication.[14]

The paranoid style involves an important populist element that resonates with the Trumpian message of a self-serving "elite" diametrically opposed to the common people. For climate change deniers, this elite includes a cabal of climate scientists, political leaders, and "deep state" government officials who perpetuate the idea of human-caused climate change. In his InfoWars broadcasts during and after Hurricane Irma's path across Florida, media host Alex Jones, admired by Trump, described this notion of a conspiratorial elite with evil designs as he talked "about the total class system of this whole secret global scientific and military industrial elite that Eisenhower warned of," concluding that "now this is the new super elite class." Although specific individuals, such as Al Gore, are frequently singled out by climate change deniers including Jones, this "super elite class" is often referred to as an amorphous but powerful "they" in the construction of alternative narratives.[15]

"They" (the conspiratorial enemy) are said to "possess some especially effective source of power." The enemy, Hofstadter explains, "controls the press; he directs the public mind through 'managed news.'"[16] In her research on the alternative media ecosystem, Kate Starbird emphasizes that the "rejection of mainstream news is a common theme across alternative media domains," which include Trump favorites like InfoWars and Breitbart News. These media outlets "explicitly set themselves up as opposition to mainstream, 'corporate' media," or what Trump has labeled "fake news."[17] In his September 12, 2017, InfoWars show, Jones explained how "they're covering it [the real truth] up in *Scientific American* and all these [mainstream] tech magazines." His guest, James McCanney, derided what he variously called the "fake weather news" and the "pretend weather news" for perpetuating what he claimed was a myth that "hurricanes are caused by warm water."[18]

Climate change deniers adopt the discourses of critical thinking and science to construct their alternative narratives. Starbird and danah boyd[19] both note how media outlets like InfoWars appropriate arguments about media literacy, instructing the audience to be skeptical about mainstream news and do their own research. In his shows about Hurricane Irma, Jones brought on a guest billed as an expert ("a famous physics professor," "the real deal") to present his own scientifically packaged explanation for the destructive power of the storm (i.e., it was geoengineered). In doing so, Jones and his guest, McCanney, adopted many of the tactics discussed by Naomi Oreskes and Erik Conway in their book *Merchants of Doubt*, including "cherry-picking data," "focusing on unexplained or anomalous details," and creating the "impression of controversy simply by asking questions" whether the answers helped their own case or not.[20]

As Jones and McCanney cast doubt on the view that the intensity of the season's hurricanes could be attributable to factors related to climate change, they presented their own case as certain ("There's no question Hurricane Irma was manipulated," said McCanney). After McCanney provided his (pseudo)scientific explanation of the way space-based lasers can be used to "drag these things [hurricanes] around," Jones concluded that the facts have been "hiding in plain view" but have been given scant attention by the mainstream media. He placed the onus on the viewers to be more skeptical.

For many, the idea that Hurricane Irma was geoengineered by an elite cabal in a secretive false flag operation to perpetuate the "hoax" of anthropogenic climate change sounds more like a parody skit or a sci-fi action film. (If you're wondering, Jones talked about the movie *Geostorm* and introduced it as further evidence in support of the geoengineering narrative.) While Alex Jones's lawyers have characterized him as "a performance artist" who is "playing a character" (perhaps akin to a professional wrestler), there is no doubt his media outlets have a real influence on views in the age of Trump—the president himself often amplifies the ideas promoted by InfoWars.

Jones epitomizes the paranoid style introduced by Hofstadter, a style that Jesse Walker claims "*is* American politics" and not merely a style practiced on the fringe.[21] Even if viewers reject the specific narrative spun on his post-Irma shows, the Alex Jones YouTube channel offered (until it was removed for violating community guidelines) other alternative climate change narratives that more realistically attempt to "use science against itself" to sow doubt and confusion.[22] This underscores the ultimate impact the paranoid style has on American politics: it breeds a form of post-truth cynicism that "can effectively shut down debate on legitimate issues by moving the discourse into the realm of ideologically distorted fantasy."[23] It destroys confidence in science as a tool for guiding thoughtful responses to issues like climate change.

Propaganda typically refers to manipulative techniques and misleading messages used to gain public acquiescence for a political cause, especially during times of war. Over the past century, George Orwell, Harold Lasswell, Jacques Ellul, and Edward S. Herman and Noam Chomsky, among others, have written or theorized about propaganda. But these approaches were developed when traditional forms of mass media represented the vanguard of message dissemination.[24]

How are we to make sense of today's propagandistic messages, which seem to increasingly occur online in the form of *fake news*? Facebook election ads created and promoted by Russian trolls; tweets that accuse students at Marjory Stoneman Douglas High School of being "crisis actors" after the mass shooting there in February 2018; a president who invents facts to bolster his worldview: these and other examples are the 21st century's version of propaganda, and they are aimed at spreading disinformation and sowing ignorance, division, doubt, and fear.

We need a 21st-century theory of propaganda to make sense of today's disinformation campaigns, whether they emanate from Russian troll farms or the Twitter feeds of the president and his cheerleaders. In his book *The Discourse of Propaganda*, John Oddo provides the theoretical purchase needed to analyze propaganda in the digital age.[25] Central to Oddo's theory is recognition that propaganda—which he defines as manipulative and anti-democratic discourse that "harms the Many and serves the Few"—involves an intertextually rich communicative process "that requires contributions from multiple agents. It can succeed in circulating only if it continually induces new audiences to recognize and recontextualize it on a mass scale." Although Oddo illustrates his theory using case studies from the two US-led wars in Iraq, the ideas are tailor-made for analyzing current events.

Propaganda ultimately relies on the recontextualization of messages to gain traction and propagate. The social media ads placed by Russian trolls are a case in point. By inducing "likes" and "shares," ads such as these hold the potential to go viral, much like the conspiracy theory tweets about students at Marjory Stoneman Douglas High School being "crisis actors."

Greg Urban points out that "some kinds of discourse are intrinsically more shareable than others."[26] What makes certain messages more prone to being propagated? Richard Bauman and Charles Briggs explain how elements of performance play an important role in "rendering discourse extractable," citing parallelism, repetition, and dramatic pauses as examples of poetic devices that make discourse more likely to be turned into easily repeatable messages.[27] In the online world, one should add that shock value enhances the intrinsic worth of tweets and posts. The more deliberately offensive or provocative a post, the more likely it will be shared. Trolls thrive off this maxim.

Propaganda must also be detachable and mobile. Social media platforms build this capacity into their technologies, making retweeting, reposting, and sharing messages easy to achieve with a simple click. Automated propaganda bots—created and controlled by human propagandists—can help circulate messages online, amplify the number of shares, and catapult messages to trending topics. Bot creators sometimes create hashtags and "use their bots to amplify them until they're adopted by human users," Erin Griffith writes in *Wired*.[28] "Over time the hashtag moves out of the bot network to the general public," explains Ash Bhat, a computer science student at the University of California, Berkeley, who helped start a project to track propaganda bots.[29]

Classical views of communication and propaganda have overemphasized both as vertical processes. In the classical view, as Debra Spitulnik describes, "there is a privileging of a one-way directionality from a mass communication form to the masses, who supposedly receive it and consume it."[30] While this may have made sense in the age of television when classical models of communication were formulated, the age of social media exposes the inherent flaws of those models.

In contrast to the vertical, Spitulnik discusses the importance of lateral forms of communication, and Oddo similarly emphasizes the importance of *horizontal propaganda*: "propaganda spread collectively by a diffusion of participants." Oddo discusses the role of deliberate vertical propagandists, but his focus on horizontal propaganda allows for unwitting actors to play a crucial role in the diffusion of messages. The humans behind propaganda bots may be involved in a deliberate campaign to disseminate manipulative messages (vertical propaganda), but the success of the campaign requires the participation of others who help to collectively circulate the messages (horizontal propaganda).

In the case of the conspiracy tweets about students at Marjory Stoneman Douglas High School, the horizontal propagandists included high-profile individuals such as Donald Trump Jr., who liked the tweets, and Rush Limbaugh and other pundits who recontextualized versions of the accusations on television. In the case of Russian-led pre-election propaganda, the *New York Times* reports, "While most of the Americans duped by the Russian trolls were not public figures, some higher-profile people were fooled."[31] Robert Mueller's indictment of 13 Russians in early 2018 mentioned how one Russian Twitter feed, @TEN_GOP, "attracted more than 100,000 followers. It was retweeted by Donald Trump Jr.; Kellyanne Conway, the president's counselor; Michael T. Flynn, the former national security adviser; and his son, Michael Flynn Jr."[32]

Lest you get too comfortable thinking you are immune from spreading misleading or manipulative messages, keep in mind that sharing outrageous messages simply to point out their absurdity—like the conspiracy theories about the high school students—helps give those messages traction. "The well-intentioned also, inadvertently, participate in the cycle of making a conspiracy theory go viral," Abby Ohlheiser reminds us in the *Washington Post*. "The thing about sharing your outrage over a despicable idea is that it's still a share."[33]

Making sense of propaganda in the age of social media requires recognizing with Oddo that "propaganda is a distributed activity—a dialogic process." In other words, "it is not quite accurate to speak of a single propagandist who intentionally delivers a self-serving message to the masses." We are all part of the intertextual web of influence that comprises our democratic society. How we use our voices in that intertextual web, though, is ultimately up to us.

6 FAKE NEWS AND MISINFORMATION

Where does the term *fake news* come from, and what does it mean anyway? When they are faced with misinformation, what is the most effective way for journalists, voters, and political fact-checkers to correct the record? The essays in this section build on the themes in the previous section, diving deeper into the meaning and use of the term *fake news* and providing a practical guide for political fact-checkers.

Recognizing that different meanings of *fake news* coexist in public discourse in the United States constitutes a necessary first step to more productive conversations about how to deal with intentionally false news stories. When it comes to correcting the record, the way journalists typically go about reporting on Trump's false claims is all wrong. Journalists should adopt an approach to political fact-checking that takes into account insights from "misconception-based learning" strategies to avoid strengthening false claims when debunking them.

Collins Dictionary named *fake news* its word of the year in 2017, an easy choice given the word's "unprecedented usage increase" of 365 percent over the previous year. *Collins* defines *fake news* as "false, often sensational, information disseminated under the guise of news."[1] But this dictionary definition belies the shifting usage of the word since the 2016 election.[2]

A poll by Monmouth University in April 2018 found that most Americans consider *fake news* to encompass not just "stories where the facts are wrong"; they also apply the word "to how news outlets make editorial decisions about what they choose to report."[3] In other words, the "fake" part of *fake news* no longer simply refers to the truth or falsity of stories. The concern with objective verifiability of facts has faded away. Now, news stories are verified in terms of how well they ideologically conform to a worldview.

The term has circulated through American political discourse since Trump took office, namely through the tweets of a president who reappropriated the term to bludgeon the free press. The term *fake news* was tweeted 403 times from the @realdonaldtrump Twitter account between December 2016 and May 2019. These tweets—most occurring after Trump moved into the White House—play an important role in shaping the word's meaning in US public discourse.

Collins Dictionary's definition of *fake news* has more to do with the meaning ascribed to the term during and immediately after the 2016 presidential election when concern about demonstrably false stories rose to the surface. This "false, often sensational, information disseminated under the guise of news" put Google and Facebook in the hot seat for the way their business models helped clickbait-scammers and Russian trolls spread false stories, whether for profit or propaganda. *Fake* in these usage contexts clearly derives from a correspondence theory of truth framework where stories that do not align with objective facts can be ferreted out and labeled *fake news*.

Well before 2016, *fake news* was better known as the moniker for the genre of satirical news shows. During George W. Bush's tenure in the White House, Jon Stewart of Comedy Central's *The Daily Show* came to be known as "the most trusted name in fake news." Stephen Colbert's spin-off show, *The Colbert Report*, took the meaning of *fake news* to a new level through his satirical caricature of a conservative talk-show host. Both of these shows drew on the comical precedent set by shows like *Saturday Night Live* with its "Weekend Update," a parodic spoof on real news broadcasts. *Fake* in these usage contexts refers to news-like shows that are obviously and transparently fake, intended for comedic entertainment and political satire.

The term *fake news* has evolved into an ideological term of art used to discredit any perceived criticism of

Trumpian demagoguery. When the term referred to propagandistic messages that favored Trump during the 2016
election, Trump took offense to the implication that he
didn't win the election on his own merits. So from the
first usage of *fake news* in his tweets, Trump effectively
reappropriated the term and twisted its meaning to protect his egocentric coherence. Throughout his body of
tweets, Trump has consistently applied the term in the
ideological sense of characterizing any news coverage at
odds with his agenda. Truth be damned.

In his tweets, *fake news* applies to both news coverage
and media outlets. For example, on January 11, 2017, Trump
tweeted in reference to reports about Russian interference
in the election: "Intelligence agencies should never have
allowed this fake news to 'leak' into the public. One last
shot at me. Are we living in Nazi Germany?" The news coverage he references also includes unfavorable polls: "Any
negative polls are fake news, just like the CNN, ABC,
NBC polls in the election."

But most importantly, in Trumpian discourse, *fake news*
has become a synonym for the mainstream media. Trump
tweets, "The FAKE NEWS media (failing @nytimes,
@NBCNews, @ABC, @CBS, @CNN) is not my enemy,
it is the enemy of the American People!" Within the
Trumpian worldview, the mainstream media consist of
newspapers like the *New York Times* and *Washington Post*—
"The Fake News Washington Post"—television networks
like ABC, CBS, and NBC, and cable news channels like
CNN and MSNBC. As Trump tweets, "The 'Fakers' at

CNN, NBC, ABC & CBS have done so much dishonest reporting that they should only be allowed to get awards for fiction!"

Notably absent, of course, is Fox News, Trump's go-to source for his daily intelligence briefings, especially the morning show *Fox and Friends*, which Trump has a symbiotic relationship with. They puff him up and he promotes them in return—for example, tweeting "Was @foxand friends just named the most influential show in news? You deserve it—three great people! The many Fake News Hate Shows should study your formula for success!"

Since the 2016 election, *fake news* has entered into the intertextual web of US public discourse where its repeated usage in contexts where real news and respected media outlets are discredited—including Trump's "Fake News Awards" spectacle in January 2018—has imbued the term with new indexical associations. But at the same time, *fake news* continues to be used in contexts where it refers to objectively false news. On the one hand, then, *fake news* means what *Collins Dictionary* says it means: "false, often sensational, information disseminated under the guise of news." On the other hand, *fake news* also means something like this: any news that contradicts Trumpian policies or affronts Trump's ego.

These different meanings operate on completely different planes of existence. One uses empirical verifiability to measure the legitimacy of news, upholding the value of a free press in a democratic society. The other uses ideological adherence to a worldview to measure the legitimacy of news, eroding trust in a free press dedicated to holding those in power accountable. These radically different usages of *fake news* render the phrase mostly meaningless in today's political debates and feed the cynicism of the Trumpian age. Using the term in this political environment requires defining what you mean by it and challenging others to do the same.

To defend his policy of separating immigrant children from their parents during the summer of 2018, Trump uttered several bald-faced lies to deflect responsibility for the humanitarian crisis he created and to falsely pin the blame on Democrats. Although the lies he and administration officials repeated seemed to represent a new nadir even for this presidency, the constant flow of misinformation from this White House has vexed political journalists from day one. How do you cover a president who frequently utters false claims without giving credence to the misinformation?[4]

The political press's answer has been to double-down on fact-checking articles to correct the record. But the way the press typically goes about this is all wrong, according to scholarly insights on how misinformation persists.[5] The key to correcting misinformation lies in creating what George Lakoff calls a "truth sandwich,"[6] or adopting what John Cook describes as a fact-myth-fallacy structure for refuting false claims.[7]

The problem with the press's standard fact-checking approach is that the refutation of lies often backfires due to the familiarity of the misinformation ("familiarity backfire effect"), the complexity of the refutations ("overkill backfire effect"), or the defensive processing of facts at odds with partisan views ("worldview backfire effect"). These "backfire" and "boomerang"[8] effects mean that the traditional fact-checking approach may even lead people to strengthen factually inaccurate understandings when presented with "preference-incongruent information."[9]

Given these impediments to countering misinformation, political journalists need to adopt a different approach to maximize the potential for setting the record straight—an approach that draws from misconception-based learning and "inoculation theory."[10] John Cook and colleagues explain that an explicit warning should preface statements of misinformation; the facts that counter misinformation need to be repeated and strengthened; and corrections need to explain why the disputed claims are erroneous.[11]

Take the example of a *Washington Post* article published on June 19, 2018, "The Facts about Trump's Policy of Separating Families at the Border,"[12] to consider how political journalists might become more effective at adopting these principles. The article, which comes from the *Post*'s coverage of the administration's false claims about its child separation policy, starts by reiterating, and thereby reinforcing, the false claims (rather than the facts). This occurs before providing a disclaimer that the claims are false and well before introducing the facts at odds with the disputed claims. The false claims are repeated and strengthened both through direct reported speech—a series of five quotes that allow administration officials to reanimate the false claims in their own voices—and indirect reported speech as the reporter paraphrases the administration's main claim. In other words, the article's opening repeats and strengthens the false claims, rather than the facts. Furthermore, the article rehearses these false claims before warning readers that the claims are false. This is a crucial misstep because the "strengthening of the initial misinformation seems to have a stronger *negative* effect than strengthening of the retraction has a *positive* effect."[13]

After the administration's claims are introduced and repeated, the article states, "These claims are false." This is a clear warning, but it is not an advance warning. The warning should precede the false claims, and both the warning and reporting of false claims should appear after a clear statement of the key fact in the case.

Next, the article explains why the administration's claims are false. This is an important move, but the explanation falls short because it delays the presentation of the key fact needed to debunk the administration's main claim. Compare the first statement below (the journalist's paraphrase of the administration's main claim) to the second statement (the key fact that refutes the administration's claim):

1. "The president and top administration officials say U.S. laws or court rulings are forcing them to separate families that are caught trying to cross the southern border."

2. "No law or court ruling mandates family separations."

When presented side-by-side, the juxtaposition of the fact in (2) with the administration's claim in (1) provides a succinct and straightforward refutation. However, in the article, this second statement does not occur until two paragraphs after the first (and again, it should occur before). The intervening paragraphs unnecessarily delay presentation of this key fact, adding layers of detail (unnecessary complexity) that distract and delay readers' ability to update their mental model of the situation.

In other words, the article starts by reinforcing an erroneous mental model (repetition of the false claims), removes a key piece of that mental model (stating those claims are false), and delays filling the resulting gap. As Cook and colleagues explain, "If a central piece of the model is invalidated, people are left with a gap in their model, while the invalidated piece of information remains accessible in memory. When questioned about the event, people often use the still readily available misinformation rather than acknowledge the gap in their understanding."[14]

Based on a similar look at other articles in the *Washington Post* and *New York Times*, this ineffective approach to debunking false claims seems to be quite prevalent in the nation's newspapers of record. Why is this so? The short answer may have to do with the nature of political reporting. The objective of journalism, after all, is to report on what is happening, which includes what the president and administration figures are saying. When those figures say things that are factually incorrect, the focus tends to remain on what they've said. The false claims are foregrounded and become the focal point while the facts needed to refute the claims get buried.

To effectively counter false claims and misinformation, factual corrections need to enter into the intertextual web of public discourse through messages that are structured for maximum effect. This requires foregrounding and repeating what is factually correct, warning readers before introducing false claims, and unpacking the fallacies that distort the facts. Although even these best practices may fall short with strident partisans, fact-checking journalists trying to set the record straight for the rest of the citizenry would be well served by adopting this fact-myth-fallacy structure for countering misinformation.

> **HOW TO COUNTER A FALSE CLAIM**
> State, repeat, and reinforce the fact.
> Warn of and point out the false claim.
> Explain how the false claim distorts.

On December 7, 2015, the Trump presidential campaign released a statement that the candidate also read (with a few extra words of emphasis) at a campaign rally in South Carolina: "Donald J. Trump is calling for a total and complete shutdown of Muslims entering the United States until our country's representatives can figure out what the hell is going on."

Seven days after his inauguration, on January 27, 2017, Trump made good on his promise by signing Executive Order 13769, titled "Protecting the Nation from Foreign Terrorist Entry into the United States." Despite the official title, the order simply came to be known as the "Muslim ban," the fulfillment of Trump's campaign promise.

The Muslim ban spawned demonstrations at airports around the United States and threw travel plans for residents of countries listed in the executive order into disarray. The order quickly landed in the courts where it was temporarily blocked and then superseded by Executive

Order 13780 on March 6, 2017. The new order, also enti-
tled "Protecting the Nation from Foreign Terrorist Entry
into the United States" and still widely recognized as a
veiled "Muslim ban," made its way through the courts
and was revised by two presidential proclamations with
the final instantiation of the policy upheld by the Supreme
Court on June 26, 2018.

Trump's call "for a total and complete shutdown of
Muslims entering the United States" gave explicit voice
to the implicit anti-Muslim sentiments underpinning the
Bush administration's so-called war on terror. The essays
in this section probe how Trump's demonization of Muslims and his conflation of a religion with violent terrorist
organizations like ISIS elevates Bush's "war on terror"
narrative to its logical extreme. Countering the anti-
Muslim sentiment stoked by that narrative starts by
resisting the stigmatization of the Islamic faith through
the pejoration of words and phrases like *Allāhu akbar*, an
Arabic phrase that holds important religious significance
for the nearly two billion Muslims worldwide.

HAS ISIS FOUND ITS PERFECT FOIL IN DONALD TRUMP?

For all the talk about identity politics and the 2016 presidential election, not enough has been said about the way identity fuels global conflicts, including the one in which ISIS has become a central player. But the success of the ISIS brand depends on an identity-oriented recruitment campaign to which any government seeking to formulate an effective response must give serious thought. Others have written about the way policies feed into ISIS recruitment, but I want to focus here on why that is the case from an identity perspective.

Scholars interested in identity and interaction recognize that, no matter how much we like to view identities as static, preexisting categories, identities ultimately emerge through sociopolitical interaction. We stake out identity positions through both positive identity practices to define who we are—for example, "Americans are advocates of free speech and human rights"—and negative identity practices to define who we are not; for example, "Americans are not torturers or unreliable trade partners."

Central to these identity practices are the two poles of identity: sameness and difference. To create an in-group with a common identity, elements of sameness are emphasized among members of the group (while differences are downplayed). At the same time, the in-group identity takes shape by highlighting differences between it and an out-group (while downplaying differences among members of the out-group).

Sociocultural linguists Mary Bucholtz and Kira Hall use the terms *adequation* and *distinction* to refer to these complementary tactics. The term *adequation* implies a certain amount of adequacy to the process of equating members of an in-group. As Bucholtz and Hall write, members of the in-group "need not—and in any case cannot—be identical, but must merely be understood as sufficiently similar for current interactional purposes."[1] To create a unified American identity position, for example, internal political differences are set aside as shared traits between Democrats and Republicans are emphasized. The flipside of adequation is the tactic of *distinction* whereby differences between two groups are brought into sharp relief to differentiate one from another. Democrats and Republicans are often differentiated, for example, through their divergent stances on tax policy or the role of government.

This underscores how any given identity position requires competing and interacting identity positions to give it meaning. A teacher's identity, for example, comes to exist only in relation to a student's identity. In this way, the identity position of one group relies upon a web of (often contested) social interactions that position it in relation to other groups. We see this play out in fictional dramas where protagonists take on identity positions in opposition to antagonists. Batman goes up against his nemesis, the Joker. Luke Skywalker battles Darth Vader. For any drama to be worth watching, we need a villain to act as the hero's foil. We take great pleasure in watching a character contrast with and enhance the qualities of another.

ISIS recruitment feeds off its own apocalyptic narrative, which requires an arch rival to act as its foil. Within the narrative, the collective "West" (comprised of the United States and many European nations) fulfills that role. Al-Qaeda first outlined the narrative that was then ratified by President George W. Bush in his own "war on terror" narrative, setting up a dualistic battle between good and evil.[2] Osama bin Laden never ceased to frame his cause as a religious war, and now ISIS spokesmen go to great lengths to position the West as involved in a war against Islam.

Bush treaded carefully to avoid casting his "war on terror" as a religious war per se; he uttered the word "crusade" once after 9/11 and steadfastly avoided the term thereafter, and in numerous speeches he attempted to distinguish between Islam and Al-Qaeda. President Obama dropped the "war on terror" language altogether, even as he continued the militarized response to terrorism initiated by the Bush administration. But with Donald Trump in the White House, ISIS finally found its perfect foil: a reality-TV star willing to play the role of its arch nemesis in "a war between Islam and the West."

Donald Trump is the perfect foil for ISIS because he steps wholeheartedly into the identity position created for him within the ISIS narrative. His executive order to bar entry of citizens from seven Muslim majority countries along with his pronouncement to favor Christian refugees over Muslims fleeing Syria couldn't have been better played by a caricature conjured up by the creators of *South Park*.

Through his pronouncements, Trump contributes to the tactic of distinction that fuels ISIS identity and feeds its apocalyptic narrative of a war between the West and Islam, Christians versus Muslims. Through the tactic of adequation, Trump's white nationalist rhetoric erases the diversity within US society, positioning America as a homogenous Christian nation at war with the Islamic State. Through his rhetoric, he lumps together Muslim Americans as part of an undifferentiated Muslim "other" and adequates the Islamic State with Islam the religion. Whether Donald Trump truly believes everything he says or whether it's just another ratings-obsessed reality-TV role for him, he seems to have convinced many in his own party to play along with the performance.

In May 2017, President Trump embarked on his first international trip since moving into the White House. Each day leading up to his departure brought a fusillade of damning reports about his fitness for office, especially after Special Counsel Robert Mueller was appointed to investigate his campaign's ties to Russia and concerns about obstruction of justice. All eyes turned to how Trump would comport himself overseas.[3]

What would the man who initiated a "Muslim ban," embraced the term "radical Islamic extremism," and peddled the totalizing view that "Islam hates us" say at a major address to Arab and Muslim leaders in Saudi Arabia? As it turns out, Trump delivered a speech that not only attempted to take the advice of his new national security advisor, H. R. McMaster—namely, to avoid the term "radical Islamic terrorism"—but also adopted some of the distinct themes of the Bush "war on terror" narrative to formulate his message on terrorism.

On the advice of McMaster, the Trump team attempted to replace his preferred terms "radical Islamic extremism" and "radical Islamic terrorism" with "Islamist extremism" and "Islamist terror groups"—in other words, opting for *Islamist* over *Islamic* to avoid broadly denouncing the entire Islamic faith. At least those were the terms written in his prepared remarks.[4] In his actual remarks,[5] he talked of "confronting the crisis of Islamic extremism and the Islamists and Islamic terror of all kinds," using both *Islamists* and *Islamic extremism/terror*. The *New York Times* cited an aide who chalked up the discrepancy to "an exhausted guy," claiming that Trump "had tripped over the term, rather than rejected the language suggested by his aides."[6]

Exhaustion appeared elsewhere in the Saudi Arabia speech as Trump attempted to move away from his rhetorical war against Islam. He adopted the reasoning of President George W. Bush, who often emphasized "that the war against terrorism is not a war against Muslims," that it is "a war not against a religion, not against the Muslim faith."[7] Despite stumbling over the prepared remarks, Trump conveyed the idea that "this is not a battle between different faiths, different sects, or different civilizations."

His prepared remarks went on to claim, "This is a battle between barbaric criminals who seek to obliterate human life, and decent people of all religions who seek to protect it." But Trump introduced a small intertextual gap during his performance to instead say, "This is a battle between barbaric criminals who seek to obliterate human life and decent people, all in the name of religion—people that want to protect life and want to protect their religion." His delivery missed the opportunity to rhetorically unify "all religions" against the "barbaric criminals," but the basic message holds that it is not "a battle between different faiths."

But if not a battle against religion, then a battle against what? Throughout the speech, Trump further channeled Bush to present the battle as an ideological struggle. In his "war on terror" narrative, Bush readily framed the conflict as akin to the struggles against "all the murderous ideologies of the twentieth century," branding it "the decisive ideological struggle of the twenty-first century," and referring to the "murderous ideology of the Islamic radicals."[8] For his part, Trump took this theme of an ideological struggle and, with his fondness for gratuitous modifiers, spoke of the "wicked ideology," "craven ideology," and "violent ideology" of terrorists. Two days later in Israel, Trump added "hateful ideology" and "evil ideology."

Evil, rather than a frivolous adjective, represents a major theme in both Bush's and Trump's descriptions of the struggle. As Bush frequently exhorted, "We're taking action against evil people." "It's a war against evil people who conduct crimes against innocent people." "Our war is a war against evil. This is clearly a case of good versus evil, and make no mistake about it—good will prevail." Likewise, Trump plainly stated, "This is a battle between good and evil," and called terrorists "the foot soldiers of evil" as he continued to embrace the dualistic division of the world established in Bush's "war on terror" narrative. Despite efforts to play down the conflict as one between religions, the religious connotations of "good versus evil" in the language remain.

Annita Lazar and Michelle Lazar coined the term *(e)vilification* "to highlight a particular and powerful kind of vilification, one based upon the spiritual/religious dichotomy between 'good' and 'evil.'" They explain, "As a strategy of out-casting, (e)vilification effectively banishes the other from the moral order that is fundamentally good and godly, and invokes a moral duty to destroy that evil."[9]

Although Trump has not adopted Bush's "war on terror" moniker to refer to the conflict, he follows the good versus evil binary to its destructive conclusion as he rhetorically embraces an ideologically driven war of annihilation. As Trump said in Bethlehem a few days after leaving Saudi Arabia, "This wicked ideology must be obliterated—and I mean completely obliterated,"[10] or as Trump emphasized in his inauguration speech, "eradicate[d] completely from the face of the earth."[11] Of course, in his inauguration speech, Trump spoke of eradicating "radical Islamic terrorism," a term that, at least on this trip abroad, he tried to avoid while looking to Bush's established terrorism narrative to articulate his own administration's doctrine.

But in his scripted speeches—and especially in his unscripted remarks—Trump is no Bush. He found his own new term of art to replace his previously preferred but problematic one. As he reacted to the tragic bombing that took place in Manchester on May 22, 2017—a terrorist bombing that claimed 23 lives and wounded 139 as they left an Ariana Grande concert—Trump chose to call the ISIS-linked perpetrators "evil losers." He elaborated, "I will call them from now on losers because that's what they are. They're losers." With that, Trump may have made his most sensible promise yet.

Allāhu akbar, the Arabic phrase meaning "God is the greatest," has gained connotations in US public discourse that differ vastly from its meaning among Muslims. Understanding how phrases like this one undergo semantic pejoration to acquire unfavorable connotations may be the first step to reclaiming its positive meaning. Doing so holds particular import at a time when a US president stokes anti-Muslim sentiments at home and abroad.[12]

I spent four academic years between 2014 and 2018 living and teaching in Qatar, a Muslim-majority nation located on a peninsula the size of Connecticut that juts into the Persian Gulf north of Saudi Arabia. One of the things I enjoyed most about my time there was going for a walk around sunset as the evening call to prayer sounded from the minarets of the local mosques. In the dusty sky of the Arabian Desert, the sun would enlarge into a big orange ball that slowly eased over the western edge of the horizon. As soon as it disappeared, the melodious voice of the *mu'athin*—the person who recites the call to prayer—would begin.

Allāhu akbar. The phrase holds important religious significance for the nearly two billion Muslims worldwide. It is as ubiquitous in daily life for Muslims as *amen* or *praise the Lord* for Christians. The *mu'athin* sings a cappella through the loudspeaker affixed to the top of the minaret, lingering on each syllable of *Allāhu*—the *u* marks the nominative case of *Allah* (God). Not just anyone can become a *mu'athin*. This layperson typically possesses a gifted musical voice. He (and the public *mu'athin* is typically a man in conservative Islamic tradition) must also possess appropriate religious knowledge to lead the call to worship.

Soon neighboring mosques would start their own *athan* (call to prayer). *Allāhu akbar*. The warm evening air of the Arabian Desert, now relieved of the direct heat of the sun, would fill with an a cappella round calling everyone within earshot to the nearest mosque—and every neighborhood has a mosque within walking distance. I am not Muslim, but I savored the numinous quality of this experience as I took my evening walks after busy days.

Due in large part to those experiences, I associate *Allāhu akbar* with beauty, peace, tranquility, gratitude, compassion, and divinity. But the phrase *Allāhu akbar* has undergone semantic pejoration in US public discourse, where it has become associated with acts of terrorism. In the New York City truck attack that took place in October 2017, news reports noted that the suspect "jumped out of his truck and ran up and down the highway waving a pellet gun and paintball gun and shouting 'Allahu akbar.'"[13] After the Orlando nightclub shooting in 2016, then candidate Donald Trump tweeted, "Orlando killer shouted 'Allah hu Akbar!' as he slaughtered clubgoers."

A quick search in the *New York Times* brings up no shortage of headlines featuring the phrase: "Man with 4-Foot Sword Shouted 'Allahu Akbar' outside Buckingham Palace, Police Say" (August 26, 2017); "Assailant at Israel Embassy in Turkey Shouted 'Allahu Akbar': Turkish Police" (September 21, 2016); "Police: Man Shouts 'Allahu Akbar' in Australian Knife Attack" (August 24, 2016); "FBI Investigates Attack; Suspect Shouted 'Allahu Akbar'" (August 23, 2016); and "Man Yelling 'Allahu Akbar!' Wounds Two Belgian Police in Machete Attack" (August 6, 2016).

In American or European contexts, *Allāhu akbar* conspicuously occurs in reportage of terrorism events while remaining largely absent in the mundane discursive routines of non-Muslims and non-Arabic speakers. Repeating the phrase to characterize the terrorist affiliations of mass murderers imbues it with those negative associations. As Penelope Eckert explains, "A word's denotation can absorb connotations through association with aspects of the context in which it is used."[14] *Allāhu akbar* comes to index terrorism in the minds of many Americans and Europeans due to the shear repetition of the phrase in the context of acts of terrorism.

Some might argue that terrorists who utter the phrase before committing violent acts are responsible for imbuing it with negative connotations. But that is only part of the equation. Terrorists' use of the phrase represents but one violent context out of the hundreds of overwhelmingly positive contexts in which the phrase is uttered daily by Muslims. Instead, primary responsibility for the pejoration of *Allāhu akbar* lies with the singular focus in US public discourse on the phrase's use by violent actors.

The pejoration of *Allāhu akbar* gains momentum through its usage in news headlines and reports of violence—a usage that mirrors the anti-Muslim sentiment promoted by exclusionary Trumpian policies like the Muslim ban. Efforts to reclaim *Allāhu akbar* require explicitly defining the phrase for non-Muslim or non-Arabic-speaking audiences. To these ends, Ahsan M. Khan defines the phrase in a letter to the *Los Angeles Times* as follows: "'Allahu akbar' is not a chant of violence or warfare. It is not a call to kill others in the name of Islam. To the contrary, it is a beautiful Arabic phrase that translates to 'God is great.'"[15]

Efforts to reclaim *Allāhu akbar* also require displacing the overwhelmingly negative connotations in US public discourse by highlighting the phrase's association with positive events from everyday life. Wajahat Ali emphasizes in a *New York Times* op-ed piece that the phrase can be used "to express just the right kind of gratitude in any situation."[16] In her *Los Angeles Times* letter, Khan adds that *Allāhu akbar* "is meant to be recited when we hear good news" and she enumerates several contexts in which it might be spoken:

> I recited it at my wedding, when I got my first job and at the birth of my children. As a physician, I often say it when my patients get better from a treatment. I even recite it when

my favorite sports team wins. And I said it upon hearing the news that New York police officers were able to prevent additional casualties by neutralizing the attacker swiftly [in the NYC truck attack in October 2017].

For me, I say *Allāhu akbar* when I watch a spectacular sunset that represents all the beauty in this world.

Trump campaigned for the presidency on the promise to "Make America Great Again." His campaign came during the final years of President Barack Obama's tenure as the first African American in the Oval Office. It is no coincidence that Trump spent substantial energy during Obama's presidency promoting conspiracy theories aimed at undermining Obama's legitimacy as a US citizen. In many ways, Trump's role in the "birther" movement—so called because it fueled false claims that Obama was born in Kenya and supposedly faked his birth certificate—set the stage for his own racist campaign and presidency. For many, his call to make America great again is a veiled reference to returning America to a time when African Americans were deemed neither full citizens nor legitimate holders of political office.

As Ta-Nehisi Coates argues in his postmortem analysis of Trump's electoral college victory,[1] Trump's racist campaign themes were central to his success rather than incidental to it. Trump rose to the presidency by exploiting racist under-currents alive and well in US society. The essays in this section explore those racist undercurrents, teasing out the ways many Americans define—accurately or not—racism. From the 2016 vice presidential debates where Mike Pence eschewed the relevance of implicit racial bias in policing, to Trump's visibly racist remarks on immigration policy, to the history of racism in US society, the essays expose the assumptions and misconceptions about racism that often underpin public discourse on the topic. These essays hold implications for how to conduct more productive conversations about race and racism, conversations needed as much as ever during and after a presidency that has exposed and exploited racial divisions for political gain.

During the vice presidential debate between Tim Kaine and Mike Pence in October 2016, moderator Elaine Quijano brought up the "issue of law enforcement and race relations."[2] Only a few weeks earlier, Keith Lamont Scott had been killed in North Carolina, becoming yet another African American man to lose his life at the hands of police. Pence objected to Hillary Clinton's acknowledgment that the incident represented (in Pence's words) "an example of implicit bias in the police force."[3]

Pence's response and the exchange that followed represents one of the most consequential racial divisions in US society: the disparate understandings of what the very concept of racism means. The exchange illustrates how our society's guiding narratives about race preserve a woefully inadequate and overly narrow understanding of racism—as evidenced by the umbrage taken by Pence to the notion "that there's implicit bias in everyone in the United States." That narrow understanding of racism serves to maintain a social system where both white privilege and racial inequities remain largely invisible or at least easily ignored by many white Americans.

The dominant understanding of racism views it in individualist terms, confining it to an individual's "beliefs,

intentions, and actions," as Jane Hill describes.[4] This understanding reduces racism to personal prejudice and results in
the illusion that racism simply involves overt acts of bigotry
and easily recognizable hate crimes; it brands those responsible as societal outliers and their actions as anomalies.
Once offenders are identified, the rest of society can absolve
itself from moral responsibility and continue to pretend
that racism has little to no bearing on contemporary society. After all, don't we all celebrate MLK Day and despise
the Jim Crow era? How could we possibly be part of the
problem of racism? I'm not prejudiced, so the reasoning
goes for many white Americans.

The common refrain in defense of authorities responsible
for racially biased killings is "race had nothing to do with it."
Something else has always led to the incident. Something,
anything, but race. In the shooting of Trayvon Martin, it was
the hoodie that made him look "suspicious." In the case of
Michael Brown, it was his size—he was like "Hulk Hogan,"
described the shooting officer in an interview on ABC.[5] And
then there is the presence, whether actual or imagined, of a
gun, which may sometimes just be a wallet masquerading as
a gun, as in the case of Amadou Diallo. As the lawyer of the
Minnesota police officer who shot Philando Castile stated,
"The shooting had nothing to do with race and everything
to do with the presence of that gun," referring to the gun
that Castile was licensed to carry (and, incidentally, informed
the officer he was carrying, according to the testimony of his
girlfriend, who witnessed the shooting).[6]

In these narratives, race is an element that can somehow
be detached and separated from police-citizen interactions.

It can be willfully ignored so that the officers do not see race. For if they were to see race, according to the dominant understanding of racism, they might be "racists" and lumped together with all those anachronistic societal outliers we see on the TV and movie screen—Archie Bunker bigots and KKK wizards in pointy hats. But as author Ta-Nehisi Coates sardonically writes, "There are no racists in America, or at least none that the people who need to be white know personally."[7] So the guiding narratives go into overdrive to explain away the interactions as having nothing to do with race, and the notion of racial bias becomes anathema to those explanations.

This colorblind myth belies the research done by social psychologists—such as Jennifer Eberhardt and Phillip Atiba Goff, among others—on the implicit biases we all carry around as we interact in an American society historically shaped and culturally conditioned to categorize the world in racial terms.[8] This body of research has repeatedly demonstrated that our ability to see an object that someone is holding as a weapon, or to shoot someone actually holding a weapon, is more likely when that someone is black. In other words, race has everything to do with it. And one need not be a card-carrying member of the KKK—or even be white—to hold these culturally conditioned racial biases. But if there is any hope of keeping those biases in check, we must first acknowledge their reality and embark on a cultural project to revise the guiding narratives that sustain them.

Our dominant narratives are difficult to dislodge largely because they sow a willful blindness, or what philosopher Charles Mills terms *white ignorance*—that is, an *ignor*ing of the way systemic racism shapes the lived experience of many people of color.[9] Mills does not mean to say that white ignorance is confined to white Americans nor that all whites necessarily suffer from the affliction, but rather that this failure to see the structural and institutional aspects of racism serves to entrench the power relations that maintain white privilege and reproduce racial inequality in our society.

In many ways, white ignorance forms the bedrock impediment to broadening the popular understanding of racism. White ignorance feeds off the narrow, individualist view of racism, blinding people from seeing racism as a system of power. The very fact that people mark the term *racism* with the qualifier *systemic* when talking about that system of power underscores the privileged position that the limited, narrow understanding of racism holds within the public discourse. Racism, as a system of power, excels—just like any system of power—at obscuring both the inequities it sows and the rewards it provides to those differently positioned within the system. After all, the entrenchment of racial disparities requires that those who benefit most from being at the top of the racial hierarchy remain oblivious to the injustices experienced by those at the bottom.

Only once we all agree that racism means systemic racism—and acknowledge the reality of implicit bias—can meaningful progress be made to reform the justice system and ensure that Black Lives Matter. This was the case before Donald Trump became president and will remain the case after he leaves office.

Has the racism underlying Trump's candidacy and presidency ever been in doubt? He rehearsed racist stereotypes about Mexican immigrants during the Republican primaries and then surrounded himself with advisors who helped him run on a white nationalist platform. Once in office, he launched a commission widely seen as a veiled attempt at minority voter suppression and appointed an attorney general—Jeff Sessions—whose record on race previously disqualified him for a position on the federal judiciary. When Trump planned to visit the opening of the Mississippi Civil Rights Museum in December 2017, the NAACP urged him to skip the ceremony in light of his abhorrent record on civil rights.[10]

There may be no American president since the days of Jim Crow who has done more to foster the ideals of white supremacy. One need only look at Trump's record to draw that conclusion.[11] But our national discourse on this topic often gets simplified to that singular question: Is he a "racist"?

Trump launched another media firestorm surrounding this question when negotiating the Deferred Action for Childhood Arrivals (DACA) legislation with senators in January 2018. Trump reportedly disparaged Haiti and African countries, "demanding to know at a White House

Meeting why he should accept immigrants from 'shithole countries' rather than from places like Norway."[12] Typically, the obsessive focus placed on racist utterances deflects attention from issues of systemic and institutional racism. But in placing a visibly racist tint on Trump's immigration stance, did his remarks do more to draw attention to his administration's racist policies in this case?

Building on Jane Hill's work on the everyday language of white racism,[13] I have investigated a common discursive routine that underlies much of our talk about race and racism in US society: *the hunting-for-racists language game*.[14] I borrow the metaphor of "hunting for racists" from sociologist Eduardo Bonilla-Silva who uses the phrase to describe how the common approach to race relations involves "the careful separation of good and bad, tolerant and intolerant Americans."[15] Philosopher Ludwig Wittgenstein uses the notion of a language game to emphasize how a word takes on different meanings depending upon the activity in which it is embedded.[16] Within the hunting-for-racists language game, the concept of racism narrows to simply mean individual bigotry or personal prejudice. Racism comes to be located solely in the minds of individuals who are positioned as societal outliers. These moves support the premise that racism is a thing of the past and elide from view the systemic and institutional racism that continues to structure US society.

Interestingly, the hunting-for-racists language game "minimizes racism" while ostensibly engaging in a type of antiracist discourse that attempts to identify "racists." However, by reducing racism to individual bigotry, the discourse shifts focus onto "individual psychological dispositions"[17] or "individual beliefs and psychological states,"[18] and away from viewing racism as a system of power that requires everyday actions and institutionalized policies to remain in place. In the case of Trump's disparaging words about Haiti and African nations, it is easy to lose sight of the larger issues as everyone attempts to figure out whether he is psychologically stable and truly possesses the heart of a bigot. Or maybe not.

If there is something positive to be gleaned from his offensive words on this occasion, it is that they forced his supporters and critics alike to grapple with the racist implications of what it means to allow immigrants from Norway while seeking to deny immigrants from Haiti and African countries. Yes, reactions focused intensely on his "vulgar comments," the label for the remarks used by media outlets like National Public Radio and the *New York Times*. But at the same time, we also saw how those words connected to his demand "to know whether Haitian immigrants could be left out of any deal" on DACA and to the racially based immigration policy that Trump sought more generally.[19] That is, the obviously racist language, in this case, may have helped bring greater attention to his white supremacist policies.

Although the white supremacy implicit in those policies has been evident from the start, the racist underpinnings of the policies can be easily masked in statements like the one made by White House spokesperson Raj Shah in the wake of the incident: "Certain Washington politicians choose to fight for foreign countries, but President Trump will always fight for the American people," he said. Anodyne comments like these conveniently allow Trump allies (no matter how reluctant) to hide behind the veil of plausible deniability as they enable the racist system enacted and perpetuated by Trump administration stances and policies.

When the racism appears in visibly "vulgar" remarks, it forces reluctant Trump supporters to either begin to consider the policy implications or reach for vexed excuses. Tragically, Trump's presidency seems to be breeding more of the latter, along with a greater acceptance of overt racism in many forms. But if there is any silver lining to Trump's racist diatribes, it may be in the opportunities they provide to expose the entrenched racism that undergirds his policies. In other words, as long as the discourse doesn't get bogged down in that singular question of whether or not he is a bigot, there is an opportunity to leverage the focus on his remarks to unmask the way "everyone in his administration . . . is participating in systemic racism," as William J. Barber II, a member of the NAACP's national board, told the *Washington Post*. "We've got to get beyond the antics and address the policy."[20] Perhaps Trump's own words can help us do that.

WHAT "TYPES OF RACISM" DOES TRUMP RECOGNIZE?

In August 2017, after the deadly Unite the Right rally in Charlottesville, President Trump issued a condemnation plagued by his signature self-contradictory prevarication: "We condemn in the strongest possible terms this egregious display of hatred, bigotry, and violence—on many sides, on many sides." A year later, in August 2018, Trump was at it again, tweeting: "The riots in Charlottesville a year ago resulted in senseless death and division. We must come together as a nation. I condemn all types of racism and acts of violence. Peace to ALL Americans!" Although Trump's latest dog whistle may not be as clearly audible as the previous year's message, it holds an equally troubling dehistoricized view of racism that is willfully blind to social power. The tweet gives another nod and wink to white supremacy while wrapping itself in ostensibly anti-racist language.[21]

To unpack the message, we must ask what types of racism Trump has in mind when he condemns "all types of racism." *Jim Crow racism* enforced legal segregation across the United States from the 1880s through the civil rights era of the 1960s. Jim Crow laws replaced the Black Codes put in place by the Confederate states at the end of the Civil War. Black Codes allowed local authorities to arrest

African Americans for minor infractions and sentence them to involuntary labor, effectively reinstating a system of slavery while denying legal rights. With the passage of the 14th Amendment in 1868, which required equal protection under the law, Jim Crow laws replaced the Black Codes to provide an updated version of racial discrimination. Overt acts of bigotry, hatred, and discrimination marked the Jim Crow era, manifesting in lynching, antiblack violence, voter disenfranchisement, and other expressions of white supremacy aimed at imposing an inferior status on blacks.

Jim Crow racism drew from *scientific racism* to rationalize racial inequality and justify discrimination. From its beginning in the 18th century, scientific racism was more pseudoscience than science, coupling appeals to scientific authority with flawed methodologies and erroneous assumptions that linked physical traits and intelligence to racial categories. Races were thought to be discrete biological categories, an erroneous understanding of human differences that has persisted in the popular imagination despite scholarly recognition that human differences exist on a cline. Early physical anthropology played a role in perpetuating scientific racism, continuing well into the 20th century. But modern anthropology, led by the work of Franz Boas,[22] began to challenge scientific racism and has gone on to contribute substantial scholarly work on the concept of race and workings of racism.

After the civil rights movement won gains against legal discrimination in the 1960s, the overt racism of the Jim Crow era gave way to new forms of racism that have become subtler and more covert—operating alongside the outward endorsement of racial equality across the political spectrum. In *symbolic*, or *modern racism*, whites indirectly express racial prejudice through a moral discourse focused on values (e.g., individualism, hard work) rather than direct expressions of racial antipathy.[23] Relatedly, in *laissez-faire racism*, whites take a hands-off approach to dealing with racial inequalities while blaming African Americans for the failure to end racism.[24] Even those who sympathize with victims of past racial injustices may exhibit *aversive racism*, in which they harbor feelings of uneasiness toward minorities and experience anxiety around them.[25]

Scholarship on these new forms of racism provides insight into the way racism operates at the level of the individual, but this focus on "individual beliefs and psychological states"[26] remains primarily concerned with personal prejudice rather than *systemic racism*.[27] Viewing racism as a system of power requires looking beyond the mental states of individuals to understand the way *institutional racism* perpetuates historical patterns of discrimination from one generation to another—from slavery to Jim Crow to modern racism—in defense of white privilege.

Race in modern US society figures into the exercise of social power through the central frames of *colorblind racism*.[28] Those frames involve an embrace of abstract liberalism (e.g., "equal opportunity for all") while minimizing racism ("society has moved beyond race") to characterize current racial inequalities as natural outcomes ("that's just the way things are") resulting from "cultural differences" (as opposed to biological differences per scientific racism).

Trump doubtfully had in mind all of these "types of racism." The one exception is old-fashioned Jim Crow racism, which still shapes popular understandings by foregrounding overt racist acts perpetrated by bigoted individuals. Trump's tweet echoes popular discourse by implicitly reducing racism to personal prejudice and bigotry (rather than recognizing it as a historically situated system of power). Drawing from this definition, Trump's multiple "types of racism" allude to various permutations of racial prejudice (antiblack, antiwhite, etc.), ignoring the way racism in US society developed historically, operates systemically, and continues to shape the power relations between whites and nonwhites in domains that include, but are not limited to, education, policing, and housing.[29]

In other words, Trump's tweet dismisses the lived reality of systemic racism by signaling that perceived antiwhite discrimination (so-called reverse racism)[30] is on a par with racial injustices carried out in defense of white privilege. The tweet does this wrapped in ostensibly antiracist language drawn from the colorblind frame of abstract liberalism to lay claim to an "equal opportunity" stance against racism. But this façade presumes a symmetry that does not exist.[31] The problem is that the message fails to conceptualize racism as anything other than a decontextualized form of personal prejudice unconnected to current and historical power relations in US society.

The Trump presidency has mobilized an ardent political resistance and has also perplexed that resistance. How do you oppose a politician who operates outside so many political norms? How do you argue against reckless provocations? How do you resist normalizing the abnormal when the abnormal becomes part of everyday politics?

The essays in this section suggest some answers to these questions, arguing that the most powerful acts of resistance require more than simply shouting louder than your opponent. Effective resistance requires entering debates with a positive vision of what should come. Staying silent in the face of abhorrent behavior is a recipe for normalizing that behavior, but effective resistance also recognizes that intentional acts of silence can sometimes communicate a powerful message amid the deafening noise of a rancorous political landscape.

Although many hoped Trump's use of social media to wage ad hominem attacks would cease after he took office, even former Republican supporters, like Senator Bob Corker, have concluded that Trump has "proven himself unable to rise to the occasion."[1] Instead of the presidency changing the man, the man had changed the presidency. "I think the debasement of our nation will be what he'll be remembered most for," Corker remarked to journalists in October 2017.[2]

Corker's Republican colleague Senator Jeff Flake took to the Senate floor that same month to give his own impassioned speech in which he denounced "the present coarseness of our national dialogue with the tone set up at the top." Flake pointed to Trump's "reckless provocations" and "degradation of our politics," calling on his colleagues to "never regard as normal" the "personal attacks" and "flagrant disregard for truth and decency" that have come to mark "our current politics." Flake adjured, "We must never allow ourselves to lapse into thinking that that is just the way things are now."[3]

To extricate ourselves from this situation, we must recognize that Trump is as much a symptom as a cause of our current politics. Sure, the bully in the presidential bully pulpit has set the tone from the top with devastating consequences to our politics and our civil discourse. A poll conducted by the *Washington Post* and University of Maryland nine months into Trump's presidency found a disturbing erosion of pride in the workings of American democracy. "By and large, Americans are feeling frustrated not only with the country's politics but also their ability to talk about politics in a civil way."[4] A survey of teachers conducted by UCLA and reported by NPR in October 2017 indicated a perceived rise of incivility in classrooms as students feel "emboldened" to engage in offensive behavior.[5] As Flake summarized on the Senate floor, "Reckless, outrageous and undignified behavior has become excused and countenanced as telling it like it is when it is actually just reckless, outrageous and undignified."

But Trump is not just an agent shaping our times; he is very much a product of our times. We have long lived in a society steeped in what Deborah Tannen has called the argument culture—*argument*, that is, in the negative sense of a heated or angry fight. Tannen said she wrote her book *The Argument Culture*[6] in the late 1990s with "a sense of urgency because I believed that the moment for its message—that our public discourse had become destructively adversarial—might have peaked." But in a follow-up piece in 2013, she remarked, "How ironic that concern now seems." Her message is even more relevant during a presidency built on racial and political divisions.[7]

As Tannen contends, the root problem stems from the way we base our politics on the precept of *agonism*, a concept she borrows from Walter Ong to describe "taking a warlike stance to accomplish something that is not literally a war." Whether one looks to Carl von Clausewitz's dictum that war is politics by other means or Michel Foucault's inverse proposition "that politics is the continuation of war,"[8] we undoubtedly conceptualize politics in an agonistic manner rather than viewing war and politics as distinct human undertakings. Consider the pervasive military metaphors that litter our political discourse, from the war on the middle class to the war on Christmas. How many headlines have you read recently that mention political "battles" or policies "under attack"? As Tannen suggests, these "metaphors seep into our thinking and shape our responses."

Media coverage of politics, as Tannen points out, helps to create and reinforce "an ethic of aggression that places the highest value on attack." Trump did not create this ethic; he has merely exploited it. His waging of ad hominem attacks in 280 characters or less—551 people, places, and things insulted on Twitter, and counting, after two years into his presidency[9]—thrives off the entertainment value of negative heat: no coverage is bad coverage if it increases his Twitter following and keeps him in the spotlight. Bucking conventional trends, Trump spent far less than Clinton during the 2016 presidential election cycle but "received 15% more press coverage."[10] In large part this can be traced to the play given to attack-driven sound bites (e.g., "Lock her up!"), which in turn provided Trump "more opportunities to define Clinton than she had to define him."[11]

Trump is in the White House because our argument culture helped put him there. To ensure his tenure remains an anomaly rather than the new normal, we must replace our notion of argument as combat with the notion of argument as dialogue. In other words, we must embrace *argumentation* in the positive sense of reasoning systematically in support of ideas or actions. This advice is echoed by Krista Ratcliffe in her discussion of "rhetorical listening,"[12] Sonja Foss and Cindy Griffin in their concept of invitational rhetoric,[13] and Richard Young, Alton Becker, and Kenneth Pike in their work on Rogerian argumentation.[14] "The key," as Andrea Lunsford and John Ruszkiewicz summarize, "is a willingness to think about opposing positions and to describe them fairly."[15] Or as Trevor Noah urged during his conversation with the *New York Times* on race and identity, we need to enter debates "from a place of empathy" and "from the point of view that the person you are speaking with is a human being."[16] This starts with deep listening in a spirit of inquiry, exchanging ideas with an openness to new insights, disagreeing with respect rather than denigration, and offering ideas rather than vitriol.

Partisans may object that the other side started it and the only way to respond is, well, as Sarah Huckabee Sanders explained in June 2017—to fight fire with fire[17]—or as Trump warned in October 2017, to "fight back" in a way that "won't be pretty."[18] But employing an ethic of aggression against political opponents merely harms and degrades. We need less dogmatic insistence and more openness to genuine exploration. We need arguments that seek to gain understandings, develop ideas, critically assess options, and ultimately arrive at decisions for the common good without severing the connections between us.

Remember when everyone feared the "normalization" of a Trump presidency? Well, by March 2018 the US president could openly brag about lying to the Canadian prime minister, and his bald-faced maneuvers to discredit the Robert Mueller investigation and FBI were openly joined by House Republicans under the deceptive moniker of "oversight." Trump's attempts throughout his presidency to discredit opponents and confuse the public are nothing new. He began gaslighting America during the campaign and took that behavior into his presidency—manipulating the nation into doubting its perception of reality and replacing it with a new Orwellian normal where real news is fake and conspiracy theories are true.[19]

Trump has drawn on the same behavior to discredit the women who have accused him "of various degrees of sexual harassment, voyeurism, and assault."[20] Broader efforts to prevent the normalization of Trumpism can learn a few things by examining the dynamics of this misogyny and how the #MeToo movement has responded, including the #TrumpToo push to hold him accountable for his own history of alleged sexual harassment and assault.

Here is Trump's playbook: Deny. Misdirect. Lie. Silence. Punish. Reframe and displace allegations with his own dissembling. Invoke popular tropes (e.g., "locker room talk," "fake news") to shift the frame. Denigrate accusers with jokes about their sexual attractiveness, hand size, or IQ. Sow confusion and make people question their perception of reality. The accusations then fade away, and he is free to do the same thing all over again.

Trump silences accusers through forceful denials that confuse the public and threaten punishment. Before the election, Trump responded to allegations of sexual assault by asserting, "The events never happened. Never." Faced with questions about his own credibility, he then turned the tables on the accusers. "Every woman lied," Trump angrily declared. He followed these projections with empty but punitive promises: "All of these liars will be sued after the election is over."[21] Finally, he issued contradictory statements to make amends for the problematic behavior. "I have tremendous respect for women," Trump has repeatedly assured us.[22] The counteraccusations, punitive threats, misdirections, and contradictions silence women who have spoken out and warn others against coming forward.

Trump redefines reality by using euphemistic language and invoking alternative interpretive frames to characterize accusations of sexual harassment and assault. Before the election, he reframed his comments on the *Access Hollywood* tape as "locker room talk," displacing the more serious sexual assault frame to guide how discussants draw meaning from the incident. Within the jocular "locker room talk" frame, complaints are discursively positioned as overly sensitive or even hysterical. This frame licenses mocking behavior to win over others and enlist their help to shame, humiliate, and disparage his accusers. When women began to come forward with stories about sexual assault before the election, Trump quipped at a campaign rally, "Believe me, she would not be my first choice, that I can tell you."[23] Many supporters in the crowd laughed while others dismissed his quip as more puerile "locker room talk." Either way, the women were silenced and ignored.

To deflect accusations of sexual harassment and assault, Trump need not convince everyone that his view of reality should be believed. He just needs to sow enough confusion to dissuade and paralyze others who would otherwise speak up from doing so. In dueling stories where facts are disputed, the benefit of the doubt in a patriarchal society typically goes to the powerful man. Natasha Stoynoff, a journalist for *People* magazine, knew this when she stayed silent after an incident with Trump in 2005. Her editor at the time of the assault wrote in 2016, "The ghastly truth is that had Trump punched her, our course of action would have been much clearer."[24] But when faced with sexual assault or harassment allegations, neutral or sympathetic bystanders too often fail to listen. Many choose to remain silent because they don't know who to believe.

The #MeToo movement disrupted the taken-for-granted frame that sexual harassment and assault can be reduced to mere "misconduct" or "inappropriate behavior." Hua Hsu writes in the *New Yorker* that normalization "resides in the way that we speak, in the ideas that get refined and reworked and encoded in ordinary words until they seem harmless enough."[25] Replacing the euphemisms that powerful men like Harvey Weinstein or Donald Trump use to make their own behavior appear harmless (e.g., "locker room talk") is an important step toward resisting the normalization of that behavior. As Laura Bates emphasizes in the *Guardian*, "It's not groping or fondling—it is sexual assault."[26]

#MeToo also disrupted the cultural script in which society overwhelmingly sides with powerful men as they defend themselves against accusations of sexual harassment or assault by denigrating their accusers. Since well before Anita Hill, women—and especially women of color—have always paid the price of their own reputation and credibility for speaking about their experiences. #MeToo has demonstrated that speaking out is no longer something to be ashamed of and has pushed society to question the credibility of the sexual predators.

The more people call out intolerable behavior, the less likely that behavior will become normalized. We all need to support the courageous people who step forward to tell their stories and expose the truth, whether they are women telling their stories about Trump's misogyny or career government officials voicing their concerns about Trump's attacks on democratic institutions.

Now is not the time for the Republican leadership to remain on the sidelines, complicit in silence. "I believe the women, yes," Senator Mitch McConnell unambiguously stated in response to the allegations against Roy Moore during the Alabama Senate race in November 2017.[27] But McConnell and Representative Paul Ryan have continued to suppress their moral courage when it comes to Trump.[28] If the #MeToo movement has taught us anything, it is that sexual predators, like demagogues, profit from the quiet acceptance of abhorrent behavior. Resisting the creeping normalization of Trumpism demands following the #MeToo movement's lead and the #TrumpToo push to hold even the most powerful man in the country accountable.

Words take center stage in the verbal sparring of the Twitter age. Against the backdrop of Trumpian shenanigans and political divisiveness, speaking increasingly involves uttering more provocative or exaggerated words. Take, for example, Robert de Niro's expletive-driven denunciation of Trump at the 2018 Tony awards, followed by Trump's insult-driven response on Twitter. Pundits, politicians, and other sociopolitical actors jockey to voice their perspectives through words—whether kind or mean, well reasoned or ill conceived. Words, after all, are fundamental to human language and how we use language to engage in social interaction. But amid the endless talk and noise of today's political landscape, we often overlook the powerful communicative potential of silence.[29]

Linguists and anthropologists have long recognized the importance of silence in human communication. In his ethnography of communication of a Western Apache community, Keith Basso details several types of situations in which acts of silence, or refraining from speech, are deemed culturally appropriate and meaningful. The meaning of such acts of silence—just as with verbal acts—must be worked out in specific contexts of situation. "Although the form of silence is always the same, the function of a specific act of silence—that is, its interpretation by and effect upon other people—will vary according to the social context in which it occurs," Basso explains.[30]

Other scholars have gone on to explore the multiple discursive functions of silence.[31] Depending on the situation, silence can be negatively or positively valued. It can be interpreted as a sign of respect, as when we pause for "a moment of silence" to remember the deceased. It can be used to manage conflict[32] or to express closeness and intimacy, as in "the silence of perfect rapport between intimates who do not have to exchange words."[33] Silence can express uncertainty and distrust, defiance of authority, or solidarity.[34] Silence can be deployed to avoid speaking the unspeakable (e.g., taboo topics) or to avoid being impolite ("If you can't say anything nice, don't say anything at all"). Silence can be seen as powerlessness ("staying silent" or "being silenced") in the presence of more powerful voices, or it can be seen as an expression of power, as in the trope of the "strong silent type."

The role silence plays in the diagram of power follows Michel Foucault's "rule of the tactical polyvalence of discourses," which emphasizes the way silence—like words—is not only "both an instrument and an effect of power, but also a hindrance, a stumbling-block, a point of resistance and a starting point for an opposing strategy."[35] Anna Marie Trester, for example, illustrates the way antiwar protestors performed acts of silence to actively communicate a message of peace before and after the US invasion of Iraq in 2003.[36] In her study of the "sounds of democracy" in Nepal, Laura Kunreuther further explores

the active performance of silence as a means for protestors to "gain a voice." Kunreuther notes that "metaphors
of political voice" typically refer to verbal speech but
emphasizes that silence can be an equally valuable discursive move in democratic practice.[37]

Take, for example, Colin Kaepernick's silent image featured in a Nike ad that launched in September 2018. Kaepernick spurred NFL pregame protests against racial injustice
in 2016 by taking a knee during the national anthem and
was then blackballed by the league. As detailed in an analysis
by the *New York Times*, Kaepernick's use of silence (punctu-
ated by selective verbal speech acts) has allowed him to position his voice within the national discourse on racism in
policing—mostly without saying a word.[38] This can be seen
in the Nike ad that implicitly echoes his protest message
("Believe in something. Even if it means sacrificing everything"), his photo displayed on the cover of *GQ* magazine in
November 2017 (without an accompanying interview),[39]
and his 11,000-plus tweets (mostly retweets rather than his
own words) since then.

Kaepernick's mostly silent protest has allowed him to
communicate his message and exercise his "voice" nonver-
bally, following a protest tradition begun in 1917 with the
"Silent Protest Parade" in New York City in which several
thousand African Americans silently marched to raise
their collective voice against lynching, racial violence, and
white supremacy.[40] When Kaepernick does engage in a
verbal speech act—as with his seven-minute speech in
Amsterdam in April 2018 after receiving Amnesty Interna-

tional's Ambassador of Conscience Award—his focused words punctuate his message: "I remind you that love is at the root of our resistance. . . . A collective love that is constantly combating collective forms of racialized hate."[41]

Whereas Kaepernick's acts of silence challenge institutional power (in the form of systemic racism), Robert Mueller employed a strategy of silence backed up by institutional power (the authority of the Justice Department). From the time of his appointment as special counsel in May 2017 through the end of his investigation into Russian election interference in March 2019, Robert Mueller "granted no interviews and held no news conferences."[42] Instead, the results of his investigation, which included 34 indictments, did the speaking for Mueller—seeming to follow the maxim of "letting the facts speak for themselves." Of course, facts never do speak for themselves; rather, people speak about facts, filtering them through interpretive frames. Mueller's silence therefore allowed Trump and his supporters ample opportunities to assert control over the discourse, framing the investigation as a "witch hunt." Nevertheless, Mueller's silence exerted a powerful influence over the national discourse during the first two years of the Trump presidency. Especially in an era marked by raucous tweets and ludicrous pronouncements by the president and his lawyers, Mueller's silence exuded a gravitas that was otherwise missing from politics. Mueller's silence communicated this gravitas in large part due to the power of his office, which imbued his (silent) voice with the institutional authority of the Justice Department.

In our increasingly noisy political scene, these examples are worth remembering when contemplating how to express one's voice. Meaningful acts of silence can sometimes wield as much power as well-chosen words, effectively communicating a message that may otherwise be diluted if speakers relied on words alone.

One of the lasting legacies of the Trump presidency may very well be its impact on the federal judiciary, including the Supreme Court. On February 13, 2016, nine months before the 2016 presidential election, Justice Antonin Scalia died; and Senate Majority Leader Mitch McConnell vowed to prevent President Obama from filling the vacant seat during his final year in office. Obama nominated centrist judge Merrick Garland, but as McConnell promised, Senate Republicans refused to consider the nominee. Many assumed Hillary Clinton would become the next president, averting the long-term consequences of McConnell's gamble. But Trump's victory meant McConnell's gamble paid off and Trump would have a chance to fill Scalia's seat.

Less than two weeks after his inauguration, President Trump nominated Neil Gorsuch to the Supreme Court. Gorsuch was confirmed by the Republican-controlled Senate on April 7, 2017. Since Gorsuch, a conservative judge himself, had replaced the conservative Antonin

Scalia, the balance of the court did not change significantly, although Gorsuch, confirmed at age 49, would likely have a long tenure on the court. But on June 21, 2018, Justice Anthony Kennedy—often the swing vote on a divided Supreme Court—announced his retirement, giving President Trump an opportunity to name another conservative justice and shift the balance of the court for decades to come.

On July 9, 2018, Trump nominated Judge Brett Kavanaugh, a nominee with a decidedly partisan past. Kavanaugh worked with Ken Starr in his investigation of President Bill Clinton in the 1990s and went on to work in the George W. Bush White House. Bush nominated Kavanaugh to the US Court of Appeals in 2003 but his nomination stalled in the Senate for almost three years (due to concerns over his partisan background) before he was eventually confirmed in 2006.

The essays in this section explore issues related to the vetting of both of these Supreme Court picks. What does it mean to be an apolitical judge, as most nominees claim? What happens when that myth collides with Trumpian hyperpartisanship? The essays suggest that we need to rethink what it means to be an apolitical judge, while also recognizing that the political dimension of judging has as much to do with judicial temperament as it does judicial philosophy.

One thing Neil Gorsuch has in common with many previous Supreme Court nominees is his insistence that he is an apolitical judge.[1] Judges like to think they are apolitical[2] and merely, as Gorsuch emphasized, "follow the words that are in the law."[3] John Roberts, during his nomination hearings in 2005, likened a judge to a baseball umpire that simply calls balls and strikes.[4] Both the umpire metaphor and the insistence that judges simply "follow the words that are in the law" presume words to be transparent conveyors of meaning, and present the process of judging "as mechanical, or at most as an exercise in deductive logic."[5] The role of the judge in the interpretive process is conveniently elided from view. But ultimately, legal interpretation is an act of linguistic interpretation carried out by social actors positioned within a particular social, political, and historical context.[6]

The problem with the myth of the apolitical judge is that it is part of a discourse that relies on an incomplete set of language ideologies—that is, ideas and beliefs about language that typically operate as unrecognized assumptions—to legitimize conservative judicial philosophies. These language ideologies enter into the discourse to rationalize answers to the underlying question, *Where is meaning located?* They are incomplete because they promote certain aspects of meaning while obscuring others. Although not political in their own right, these language ideologies do important political work within the judicial confirmation process to shape the discourse and position candidates like Gorsuch within the mainstream.

The first of these language ideologies might be termed the *ideology of internalism*, based on John Thompson's[7] discussion of the fallacy of internalism—also known as the ideology of the fixed text in Jan Blommaert's adaptation of Thompson. The ideas that a text exists as "a closed, immutable unit" and that "'all' the meanings can be found in it" are central to this language ideology.[8] This ideology draws from the referentialist ideology, which holds that language use is primarily about conveying information.[9] In conveying information, language is seen merely as a conduit of meaning, as Michael Reddy describes in his critique of the conduit metaphor.[10] One person's thoughts are supposedly placed into containers (words) and "sent" to another person who opens the containers (words) to "receive" the meaning. So in response to the question about the location of meaning, the ideology of internalism locates meaning solely within the text.

The ideology of internalism is well represented in remarks made by then senator Jeff Sessions during the 2005 Roberts hearings in which he decried judges he saw as deviating from this guiding ideology: "Today many believe the law does not have an inherent moral power and that words do not have and cannot have fixed meanings."[11] On the flipside, for Sessions, "words can mean whatever a judge wants them to mean." This either-or binary set up by Sessions—that either meaning is fixed in the text or anything goes—is frequently echoed by his conservative colleagues. For example, during the 2010 Elena Kagan hearings, Senator John Cornyn asserted that if "there is no such thing as a fixed meaning of the Constitution and laws," then "judges [would] possess some sort of power to create constitutional rights out of whole cloth."[12] As seen here, senators draw from the language ideology of internalism to deny the import of context in shaping meaning.

Sometimes invoked alongside the ideology of internalism is what I will call the *ideology of intentionalism*, based on literary scholars' discussion of the intentional fallacy[13] and what anthropologists call personalism.[14] Whereas internalism locates meaning in the text itself, intentionalism locates meaning in the intentions and beliefs of the speaker or writer. To arrive at meaning, listeners or readers must calculate those intentions. As Senator Orin Hatch insisted during the 1993 Ruth Bader Ginsburg hearings, "The role of the judicial branch is to enforce the provisions of the Constitution and the laws we enact in Congress as their meaning was originally intended by the Framers."[15] Here other elements that factor into the co-construction of meaning are set aside to privilege authorial intent.

Both internalism and intentionalism can work together as part of the *baptismal ideology of meaning*, which, as Jane Hill describes, "holds that there is a single correct meaning of a word that can be found by tracing its history to an authoritative original source."[16] In line with the conduit metaphor, the authoritative original source "packages" meaning within the text and "sends" that "fixed text" to judges who then "unwrap" it to find the meaning unchanged by context. That authoritative original source might be the framers of the Constitution or legislators who write a statute. But the source could also be the "society" of the originating context, as Antonin Scalia explained during his 1986 confirmation hearings, stating that "one is bound by the meaning of the Constitution to the society to which it was promulgated," looking to "the text of the document and what it meant to the society that adopted it."[17] Here meaning is traced to the originating context of a text's creation while denying any relevance to the current interpretive context.

Hill points out that "a crucial insight of linguistic anthropology [is] that linguistic ideologies shape and constrain discourse, and thus shape and constrain the reproduction of other kinds of ideologies."[18] Although the language ideologies discussed here do not directly link to political ideologies, they do political work indirectly by supporting the types of judicial philosophies favored by conservatives, including originalism, textualism, and strict constructionism. These everyday language ideologies help rationalize conservative approaches to judicial interpretation by focalizing certain sources of meaning and discounting others. We end up with a grossly incomplete and insufficient model of meaning. Meaning is treated as fixed, transparently evident, and universally shared, while approaches that deviate from this model—for example, to account for shifting historical contexts or pragmatics—are positioned as flawed.

If one rightly agrees with Gorsuch that "words matter,"[19] one must also agree that so does history, context, and a judge's own life experiences—all of which inevitably impact the interpretive process whether recognized or not. Only then can we dispense with the myth of the apolitical judge and the pretense that all answers to legal questions have already been written and are neatly encapsulated within a "fixed text."

The myth of the apolitical judge collided with Trumpian spectacle in the confirmation hearings of the president's second nominee to the Supreme Court, Judge Brett Kavanaugh. In his opening statement on the first day of those hearings on September 4, 2018, Kavanaugh echoed Chief Justice John Roberts to underscore the idea that "a good judge must be an umpire—a neutral and impartial arbiter who favors no litigant or policy."[20] But when Kavanaugh returned before the Senate Judiciary Committee on September 27, now facing sexual assault allegations, he delivered a hyperpartisan performance that retired Supreme Court justice John Paul Stevens and other legal observers found "disqualifying" in its own right.[21]

Kavanaugh's performance belied the promise of judicial professionalism, casting doubt on the premise that a judge with a partisan pedigree like his could remain "a neutral and impartial arbiter who favors no litigant or policy." Kavanaugh abandoned the professional demeanor of a judge and turned into a partisan attack dog infected by Trumpism's virulent strain of polemics and belligerent masculinity. The performance ensured that Trumpism's legacy on the Supreme Court would revolve as much around judicial temperament as judicial philosophy.

In a skit on *Saturday Night Live* (*SNL*) a few days after Kavanaugh's performance, Matt Damon performed his own version of the angry, aggressive, and nakedly partisan Kavanaugh.[22] Damon-as-Kavanaugh entered the set scrunching his face into a scowl. He took his seat before the senators and shouted, "What!" Alex Moffat, playing Senator Charles Grassley, asked, "Judge Kavanaugh, are you ready to begin?" "Oh, hell yeah! Let me tell you this, I'm going to start at an eleven. I'm going to take it to about a fifteen real quick!" Damon-as-Kavanaugh went on to declare, "I'm here tonight because of a sham, a political con job orchestrated by the Clintons and George Soros and Kathy Griffin and Mr. Ronan Sinatra."

Damon riffed off Kavanaugh's original statement for comedic effect but also epitomized the type of paranoid style of politics indicative of Trumpism—the style Kavanaugh brought to the nomination process. In his own statement, Kavanaugh characterized his situation as "a calculated and orchestrated political hit" fueled by "revenge on behalf of the Clintons and millions of dollars in money from outside left-wing opposition groups." The conspiratorial undertones sounded like something right out of Trump's own Twitter feed.

Throughout the hearing, Kavanaugh waged a Trumpian temper tantrum as he directed anger and hostility toward the Democratic senators in the room. He interrupted their questions and at one point facetiously asked Senator Amy Klobuchar if she had ever blacked out from drinking—later apologizing for the remark that went beyond the pale of even this otherwise unapologetically combative performance.

Kavanaugh's anger at times gave way to tears, invoking an emotional tone that struck a sharp contrast to Dr. Christine Blasey Ford's solicitous and calm testimony earlier in the day. In contrast to Ford, Kavanaugh came off as a petulant bully. Writing in the *New Yorker*, Alexandra Schwartz characterized his behavior as "a model of American conservative masculinity . . . tied to the loutish, aggressive frat-boy persona." She noted how this persona has replaced "the days of a terse John Wayne-style stoicism" with one modeled by Trump, "ranting and raving at his rallies," or Alex Jones, "screaming and floridly weeping as he spouts his conspiracy theories."[23]

Kavanaugh constructed that persona by frequently invoking the drinking of beer as a masculine rite of passage. "I drank beer with my friends. Almost everyone did," Kavanaugh said. "Sometimes I had too many beers. Sometimes others did. I liked beer. I still like beer." Beer has often been a populist symbol in US politics, metonymically representing the down-to-earth sensibility of the common people. In the 2000 presidential election, voters were asked which candidate they would rather have a beer with: Bush or Gore. Bush won the beer test and went on to take the presidency.

Beer has also been a symbol of virile masculinity. One need only look at the gendered roles and stereotypes within the historical archive of television beer commercials to see how beer indexes a type of working-class masculinity now associated with Trumpian conservatism. Kavanaugh positioned himself as just another typical American male who in high school enjoyed, in his words, "working out, lifting weights, playing basketball, or hanging out and having some beers with friends as we talked about life, and football, and school and girls."

Kavanaugh staked out this identity position by using Democratic senators as a foil, daring them to deny they liked beer. As Senator Sheldon Whitehouse questioned him, Kavanaugh reiterated, "I like beer. I like beer." Then he challenged Whitehouse, "I don't know if you do. Do you like beer, Senator, or not?" As Whitehouse attempted to move on, Kavanaugh persisted, "What do you like to drink? Senator, what do you like to drink?" The questioning seemed to implicitly ask whether the Democratic senator was a real man who liked beer or an effete coastal liberal who instead drinks chardonnay, invoking the contrastive stereotypical personas of US politics.

In the *SNL* skit, Kyle Mooney, playing Senator John Kennedy, gave Damon-as-Kavanaugh a serious look and said, "Judge Kavanaugh, I only have one question for you. Look me in the eye, in front of God, and I want you to answer honestly. That beer you like to drink, are we talking foreign or domestic?" Damon-as-Kavanaugh replied, "I like American beer!" Mooney-as-Kennedy concluded, "No further questions! This guy checks out."

Likewise, Kavanaugh's performance checked out for Trump who tweeted, "Judge Kavanaugh showed America exactly why I nominated him. His testimony was powerful, honest, and riveting." White House advisor Kellyanne Conway called it "a tour de force."[24] Donald Trump Jr. tweeted, "I love Kavanaugh's tone."

In the end, Kavanaugh saved his nomination by constructing a persona for himself in line with Trump's own belligerent tone and brand of virulent polemics. But as a result, he would carry the worst aspects of Trumpism with him to the Supreme Court—male entitlement, misogyny, and bitter win-at-all-costs partisanship—while furthering the corrosive impact of Trumpism on US institutions.

Kavanaugh's performance—and the *SNL* parody of it—illustrate how identity is best viewed "as a *practice*, and as a signifying practice."[25] That practice allows individuals to construct recognizable cultural selves out of folk symbols, such as beer, imbued with sociopolitical meaning. Kavanaugh's performance also illustrates how identity construction is a relational practice that involves the "social positioning of self and other."[26] Kavanaugh positioned himself not only as a Trump acolyte in relation to liberal elites, but as a political hack in relation to professional judges.

11 MOVING PAST TRUMP

Where do we go from here? Whether future generations look back at the Trump presidency as an anomaly or the start of a lasting trend in American governance depends on how we collectively extract ourselves from this political moment and move past it.

The essays in this final section suggest that moving beyond Trump involves recognizing his lack of reliability and genuine interest in being a good-faith conversational partner in politics; then looking for ways to ensure he becomes politically irrelevant without feeding his ego or the outrage his ego spawns. The implication for candidates trying to run against Trump (or demagogues like him) is to spend as little time as possible engaging directly with the showman while focusing on more productive lines of public discourse—like defining a positive vision for the country's future. The task will be to provide a clear alternative to the politics of division and illiberalism associated with Trumpism, outlining the shared values that make democratic politics possible.

GOVERNMENT OF, BY, AND FOR THE TROLLS

The United States and the world spent the first few years of the Trump presidency trying to figure out how to deal with an antisocial president. The task holds even more import as Democrats and never-Trump Republicans consider how to challenge an incumbent president in 2020. Formulating an effective strategy should start by recognizing the ways Trumpian discourse adheres to prototypical "trolling" behavior and responding accordingly.[1]

The concept of *trolling*, first studied by Judith Donath[2] and further analyzed by Susan Herring and colleagues,[3] refers to actions by someone who baits and provokes others in online forums, "often with the result of drawing them into fruitless argument and diverting attention" away from the topics under discussion. This is similar to and often overlapping with *flaming* (actions "intended to insult, provoke or rebuke"), and in that same vein the typical troll thrives on attention, especially negative attention, which he (the troll is often a man) receives by sowing discord and instigating emotionally reactive responses. A troll is a provocateur who excels at disruption and digression, particularly when those engaging with him fail to recognize his behavior as trolling.

Trump trolls the media and citizens with tweets and statements that sow confusion and provoke futile arguments. He often achieves this by making paradoxical statements. Take, for example, his prevarication about the evidence pointing to the role played by Mohammad bin Salman (MBS), the de facto ruler of Saudi Arabia, in the premeditated murder of *Washington Post* columnist Jamal Khashoggi in October 2018. "We may never know all of the facts surrounding the murder of Mr. Jamal Khashoggi," Trump counseled in an official statement released by the White House (and what may be the first propaganda piece issued by an American president on the behest of a foreign authoritarian regime). Trump conceded that "it could very well be that the Crown Prince had knowledge of this tragic event," but then again, he opined, "maybe he did and maybe he didn't!"[4]

Later, in a Fox News interview, Trump asked rhetorically, "Who could really know?"[5] Then in an interview with the *Washington Post*, Trump reiterated, "Maybe he did and maybe he didn't. But he [MBS] denies it. And people around him deny it. And the CIA did not say affirmatively he did it, either, by the way. I'm not saying that they're saying he didn't do it, but they didn't say it affirmatively."[6] Trump "seeks to confuse and deceive, rather than to be clear," just as the troll in Susan Herring's study does. Senators later briefed by the CIA had no trouble recognizing "that this was orchestrated and organized by people under the command of MBS."[7]

Trump made similar discursive moves in his response to the Fourth National Climate Assessment (NCA4) released by the federal government in November 2018— an evidence-based report that warns of the need to take immediate action to counter the economic and health impacts of climate change. In what the *Washington Post* described as "a freewheeling 20-minute Oval Office interview," Trump went off on a tangent that touched on trash in the oceans, dirty air in Asia, and myriad topics unrelated to the central issue of climate change or the key conclusions of NCA4.

Trump's critics often characterize such stream-of-consciousness ramblings as nonsensical gibberish, but such moves are central to the troll's strategy. Delving into inconsequential minutiae barely tangential to the topic at hand allows the troll to feign sincerity at addressing the topic while he shifts the conversation toward futile arguments. Trump either misinterprets—or ignores altogether—key conclusions from evidence-based reports to shift the conversation; or he engages in strategies of denial and distortion to sow doubt on claims. In response to the conclusions of NCA4, Trump rejoined, "I don't believe it" (denial).[8] "You look at our air and our water, and it's right now at a record clean," Trump told the *Washington Post* (distortion).[9]

Interactants expect a certain level of mutual cooperation with conversational partners. But when trolls make discursive moves that obfuscate, confuse, deny, and distort, those engaging with the troll are often at a loss on how to respond because the troll's conversational contributions are so far removed from the norms. When asked by the *Washington Post* to reply to Trump's comments on NCA4, Andrew Dessler, a professor of atmospheric sciences at Texas A&M University, simply remarked, "How can one possibly respond to this?"

Trolls take pleasure in disrupting the social order and getting a rise out of others. When others do engage with the troll, it is easy to fall into a reactive response that either follows the troll down the rabbit hole of a futile or off-topic argument, or mimics the troll's inflammatory style by striking back in kind. Trolls often use "flame bait" (statements designed to inflame and infuriate) to provoke others into insult-driven tit-for-tats. Even Dessler couldn't help but label Trump's comments on NCA4 "idiotic."

So how do we deal with a president who governs by trolling?

Completely ignoring the president altogether clearly isn't an option; a viable democracy requires engagement to affect democratic accountability. And the pervasiveness of his trolling behavior makes it impossible to simply ignore or shun it. His trolling goes well beyond the people, places, and things Trump has insulted on Twitter; it seeps into every aspect of his governance, as illustrated here. Returning Trump's provocations in kind merely feeds his ego and fails to deal with the implications of his policy decisions. I agree with Michelle Obama on the need to go high "when they go low." However, trying to respond with rational counterarguments to Trump's every claim or distortion ignores the realization that trolls act as they do to deliberately steer the conversation off topic into endless inconsequential digressions. Genuine debate is not their goal. Trolls are bad-faith conversational partners, as even heated political debate requires a basic level of Gricean cooperation.

Perhaps the most important way to deal with this particular troll is to simply recognize and label his behavior as "trolling." Armed with the awareness of how a troll operates, then we can respond by not falling for the distractions, not getting stuck in a state of constant outrage, and consistently working to keep the discourse focused on the key issues at hand.

HOW A TROLL OPERATES

Uses "flame bait" to provoke reactions.

Feigns sincere desire to engage in debate.

Ignores or willfully misinterprets key points.

Bogs down debate in inconsequential details.

Sows confusion with paradoxical statements.

Fosters uncertainty with denials and distortions.

Steers debate off topic with endless digressions.

Politics and communication are fundamentally entwined, influencing one another so that the toxic discourse in the age of Trump cannot be divorced from the dysfunctional politics that mark this political moment. The dysfunctional politics we are currently experiencing may not have originated with Trump, but he became their standard bearer as he ushered in a hostile regime of language that has exacerbated that dysfunction and brought it to an ugly head.

The question then becomes how we move beyond this toxic discourse toward a more functional democratic politics. The short answer is that we must reacquaint ourselves with the cooperative principle that makes democratic politics possible, similar to the cooperative principle that makes communication possible.

Politics is often defined as the struggle for power. This view emphasizes politics as a competitive contest marked by conflict over the distribution of resources and establishment of laws. On the other hand, politics also involves people coming together to develop relationships as they work through differences, negotiate agreements, and strive toward mutual consent. This view emphasizes politics as a cooperative endeavor marked by collaboration and compromise. Politics simultaneously encompasses both of these dimensions.

Communication is not only integral to the conduct of politics but, like politics, encompasses both competitive and cooperative dimensions. On the one hand, communication—especially political communication—can be highly competitive and marked by conflict, disagreement, and debate. But just like politics, communication requires a requisite level of cooperation to make the exchange of meanings possible in the first place. To say communication is a cooperative endeavor is to recognize that even heated political debate requires a certain level of mutual cooperation to proceed.

Building on this idea that politics and political communication simultaneously involve both cooperative and competitive dimensions, imagine politics and political communication as a balance scale with cooperation and competition sitting at opposite ends of the fulcrum. In normal times, the scale may tip back and forth as weight shifts toward one end or the other; but for the most part the scale remains in a relatively dynamic equilibrium. Cooperation and competition are expressed to differing degrees at different points during the political process, but the end result is functional democratic governance.

Trumpism, however, has effectively overloaded the scale with toxic discourse, creating an unhealthy imbalance between the cooperative and competitive dimensions of democratic politics. Trumpian discourse has effectively dropped a heavy weight on the competitive end of the political scale, sending cooperation flying from the system, much like a person jumping on one end of a teeter-totter with all their weight ejects someone sitting on the other end.

In emphasizing competition while largely dispensing with cooperation, Trumpism further conceptualizes competition as a zero-sum contest with "winners" who prevail at the expense of "losers." This leads to the view of political opponents as enemies rather than good-faith political partners one might collaborate with (even if they disagree) on specific policy prescriptions. Trumpian discourse has helped shift politics toward a winner-take-all warfare model with enemies to dominate or vanquish.

The ramifications of this dysfunctional politics, which started before Trump took office but has since picked up steam, range from the refusal to hold votes on judicial nominees, to voter suppression initiatives, to partisan gerrymandering. These and other examples illustrate a win-at-all-costs mentality that seeks complete domination by engineering the system for partisan advantage rather than accepting and working within the democratic constraints and safeguards of that system.

The danger is that dispensing with cooperation altogether can lead to the marginalization of politics as a means for working through disagreements and settling competing power claims, leaving violence or even civil warfare as the only remaining recourse. But even without nearing such extremes, a politics that banishes cooperation can lead to a downward spiral of dysfunction supported by growing levels of toxic discourse.

One way to respond to Trump is to strike back in kind, to engage in hyperpartisan warfare and adopt the discursive tactics that Trump has used to rise to power—in other words, to try to out-Trump Trump. But that would be a mistake, not only from a moral perspective but also from a strategic perspective, because it fails to recognize that moving beyond this political moment requires rebalancing our politics with the requisite dose of cooperation it currently lacks.

The best antidote to Trumpism will be to reassert a core set of democratic values that have marked the US experiment in governance—the very values that Trump has violated. Those values include unconditional support of a free press, adherence to the rule of law and the idea that no person is above the law, respect for separation of powers and an independent judiciary, belief in the universal right to vote and participate in the democratic process, and yes, mutual respect and cooperation as a necessary foundation for democratic governance—civic values that Americans widely embrace regardless of party affiliation.

The next successful presidential candidate must stand for something in the affirmative rather than simply opposing Trump the man, and that candidate would do well to stand for these shared democratic values. Articulating and emphasizing those values as the bedrock of their campaign will allow them to assert a positive vision that unites, models respect, and appeals to the best in all Americans. This may be more important than any specific policy prescription they might offer, because the next successful candidate will need to forge a broad coalition of liberals, moderates, and never-Trump conservatives. The one thing that will unite that coalition is a common orientation to shared democratic values.

This is not to say that the next president will necessarily be a political moderate. But the next president will need to stand for shared democratic values that cut across traditional party lines, unite a majority of Americans around those values, and inspire a cooperative effort to make democratic governance functional again.

ACKNOWLEDGMENTS

I am grateful to Stanford University Press and Michelle Lipinski, Senior Editor, for taking on this project. Michelle, along with two anonymous reviewers, provided invaluable guidance that helped shape my initial ideas into this book. Much of the material found here was originally written for my "Trumped Up Words" column in *Anthropology News*, the magazine of the American Anthropological Association, during 2017 and 2018. I am indebted to Natalie Konopinski, Editor, and Alexandra Vieux Frankel, Assistant Editor, for the opportunity to write the column. Alexandra was especially instrumental in working with me to produce the monthly column. Many thanks to all the readers of that column who offered words of encouragement at conferences and in e-mails, convincing me that it would be worth my time to turn those essays into a book. I am also grateful to my colleagues at Carnegie Mellon University Qatar for their collegiality and to my students for all they taught me. Special thanks to my English department colleagues

Susan Hagan, Ludmila Hyman, Thomas Mitchell, Silvia Pessoa, and Dudley Reynolds. Many others have also shaped my experiences and impacted my ideas even though I cannot name them all here. I owe immense gratitude and special thanks to my partner, Sarah Vieweg, for her love and support—for helping me come up with that elusive word when the dictionary fails me, for listening to my ideas, and for putting up with my writing habits. When an idea asks me to give it voice through writing, I tend to dive underwater for hours or days at a time before coming up for air and, if all goes well, with something to share with you. Thanks for reading.

NOTES

PREFACE

1. Obama, Barack. 2016, September 20. "Final Address to the United Nations General Assembly." www.americanrhetoric.com/speeches/barackobama/barackobamaunitednations71.htm

SECTION 1: THE CYBERBULLY-IN-CHIEF

1. This essay first appeared in *Anthropology News*. Hodges, Adam. 2017. "Trump's Formulaic Twitter Insults." *Anthropology News* 58(1): e206–e211. doi:10.1111/AN.308

2. Alim, H. Samy, and Geneva Smitherman. 2012. *Articulate While Black: Barack Obama, Language, and Race in the U.S.* New York: Oxford University Press.

3. Hall, Kira, Donna Meryl Goldstein, and Matthew Bruce Ingram. 2016. "The Hands of Donald Trump: Entertainment, Gesture, Spectacle." *HAU: Journal of Ethnographic Theory* 6(2): 71–100.

4. Hall, Goldstein, and Ingram, "Hands of Donald Trump."

5. Hodges, Adam. 2014. "'Yes, We Can': The Social Life of a Political Slogan." In *Contemporary Critical Discourse Studies*, Christopher Hart and Piotr Cap (eds.), 349–66. London: Bloomsbury.

6. Lee, Jasmine C., and Kevin Quealy. 2016, January 28. "The People, Places and Things Donald Trump Has Insulted on Twitter: A Complete List." *New York Times*. https://nyti.ms/2jS6zDv

7. Mayer, Jane. 2016, July 25. "Donald Trump's Ghostwriter Tells All." *New Yorker*. www.newyorker.com/magazine/2016/07/25/donald-trumps-ghostwriter-tells-all

8. Bakhtin, Mikhail. 1981. *The Dialogic Imagination: Four Essays*, Michael Holquist (ed.), Caryl Emerson and Michael Holquist (trans.). Austin: University of Texas Press; Hodges, Adam. 2015. "Intertextuality in Discourse." In *The Handbook of Discourse Analysis*, 2nd ed. Deborah Tannen, Heidi E. Hamilton, and Deborah Schiffrin (eds.), 42–60. Hoboken, NJ: Wiley-Blackwell.

9. Kearns Goodwin, Doris. 2014. *The Bully Pulpit*. New York: Simon & Schuster.

10. This essay first appeared in *Anthropology News*. Hodges, Adam. 2017. "A Bully in the Presidential Bully Pulpit." *Anthropology News* 58(4): e282–e285. doi:10.1111/AN.569

11. "Respond to Bullying." 2012, February 29. StopBullying .Gov. www.stopbullying.gov/respond/on-the-spot/index.html

SECTION 2: THE POST-TRUTH PRESIDENCY

1. Roberts-Miller, Patricia. 2017. *Demagoguery and Democracy*. New York: The Experiment, LLC.

2. Kazin, Michael. 1998. *The Populist Persuasion: An American History*. Ithaca, NY: Cornell University Press, 1.

3. Judis, John B. 2016. *The Populist Explosion: How the Great Recession Transformed American and European Politics*. New York: Columbia Global Reports, 15. For more on these ideas as they relate to Trumpism, see: Hodges, Adam. 2019. "How Trump's Populism Shapes the Uptake of New Social Facts." *American Anthropologist* 121(1): 185–87.

4. Roberts-Miller, *Demagoguery and Democracy*.

5. Roberts-Miller, *Demagoguery and Democracy*, 79.

6. This essay first appeared in *Anthropology News*. Hodges, Adam. 2018. "A Demagogue's Words Matter." *Anthropology News*. 59(6). doi:10.1111/AN.1021

7. Santa Ana, Otto, Juan Moran, and Cynthia Sanchez. 1998. "Awash under a Brown Tide: Immigration Metaphors in California Public and Print Media Discourse." *Aztlán: A Journal of Chicano Studies* 23(2): 137–76; Santa Ana, Otto. 1999. "'Like an Animal I Was Treated': Anti-immigrant Metaphor in US Public Discourse." *Discourse and Society* 10(2): 191–224; Santa Ana, Otto. 2002. *Brown Tide Rising: Metaphors of Latinos in Contemporary American Public Discourse*. Austin: University of Texas Press.

8. Unless otherwise noted, italics are my own emphasis. They are used here to indicate metaphorical language.

9. Chilton, Paul, and George Lakoff. 1995. "Foreign Policy by Metaphor." In *Language and Peace*, C. Schäffner and A. Wenden (eds.), 37–60. Aldershot: Dartmouth.

10. Shear, Michael D., and Thomas Gibbons-Neff. 2018, October 29. "Trump Sending 5,200 Troops to the Border in an Election-Season Response to Migrants." *New York Times*. https://nyti.ms/2CRwsjp

11. Fairclough, Norman. 1989. *Language and Power*. London: Longman.

12. Roose, Kevin. 2018, October 28. "On Gab, an Extremist-Friendly Site, Pittsburgh Shooting Suspect Aired His Hatred in Full." *New York Times*. https://nyti.ms/2CNSweI.

13. Sonmez, Felicia, Michelle Ye Hee Lee, and Paul Kane. 2018, October 28. "Pence: Don't Link Political Rhetoric to Pittsburgh Synagogue Shooting." *Washington Post*. https://wapo.st/2QiVMqy

14. Kessler, Glenn, Meg Kelly, and Nicole Lewis. 2017, November 14. "President Trump Has Made 1,628 False or Misleading Claims over 298 Days." *Washington Post*. http://wapo.st/2iUoonP

15. Leonhardt, David, Ian Prasad Philbrick, and Stuart A. Thompson. 2017, December 14. "Trump's Lies vs. Obama's." *New York Times*. https://nyti.ms/2jWqBz1

16. This essay first appeared in *Anthropology News*. Hodges, Adam. 2018. "How Trump's Lying Affirms a Worldview." *Anthropology News* 59(1): e189–e192. doi:10.1111/AN.733

17. DePaulo, Bella M. 2017, December 8. "I Study Liars: I've Never Seen One like President Trump." *Washington Post*. http://wapo.st/2iDBdSh

18. Qiu, Linda, and Alicia Parlapiano. 2017, October 12. "Illegal Border Crossings Are Down, but Trump Still Exaggerates the Numbers." *New York Times*. https://nyti.ms/2kJpjtN

19. Liptak, Kevin. 2017, August 2. "Trump's Call History Called into Question." *CNN*. www.cnn.com/2017/08/02/politics/trump-phone-calls/index.html

20. Shear, Michael D., and Emmarie Huetteman. 2018, January 23. "Trump Repeats Lie about Popular Vote in Meeting with Lawmakers." *New York Times*. https://nyti.ms/2klFxo1

21. Bruner, Jerome. 1991. "The Narrative Construction of Reality." *Critical Inquiry* 18(1): 1–21.

22. Nyhan, Brendan, and Jason Reifler. 2010. "When Corrections Fail: The Persistence of Political Misperceptions." *Political Behavior* 32(2): 303–30; Hart, P. Sol, and Erik C. Nisbet. 2012. "Boomerang Effects in Science Communication: How Motivated Reasoning and Identity Cues Amplify Opinion Polarization about Climate Mitigation Policies." *Communication Research* 39(6): 701–23.

23. Bond, Charles F., and Bella M. DePaulo. 2006. "Accuracy of Deception Judgments." *Personality and Social Psychology Review* 10(3): 214–34.

24. DePaulo, "I Study Liars."

SECTION 3: POLITICAL THEATER AND SPECTACLE

1. This essay first appeared in *Anthropology News*. Hodges, Adam. 2017. "When the Discourse of Theater Trumps Truth." *Anthropology News* 58(2): e209–e213. doi:10.1111/AN.375

2. Hill, Jane. 2000. "'Read My Article': Ideological Complexity and the Over-Determination of Promising in American Presidential Politics." In *Regimes of Language: Ideologies, Polities, and Identities*, Paul V. Kroskrity (ed.), 259–92. Santa Fe: SAR Press.

3. Jakobson, Roman. 1960. "Closing Statement: Linguistics and Poetics." In *Style in Language*, Thomas Sebeok (ed.), 360–77. Cambridge: MIT Press.

4. Hall, Kira, Donna Meryl Goldstein, and Matthew Bruce Ingram. 2016. "The Hands of Donald Trump: Entertainment, Gesture, Spectacle." *HAU: Journal of Ethnographic Theory* 6(2): 71–100.

5. Clement, Scott, and Emily Guskin. 2016, November 2. "Post-ABC Tracking Poll Finds Race Tied, as Trump Opens Up an 8-Point Edge on Honesty." *Washington Post*. https://wapo.st/2fcdDK8

6. Sharockman, Aaron. 2016, October 10. "Clinton: Trump an Absolute Avalanche of Falsehoods." *PolitiFact*. www.politifact.com/truth-o-meter/article/2016/oct/10/clinton-trump-absolute-avalanche-falsehoods/

7. This essay first appeared in *Anthropology News*. Hodges, Adam. 2018. "Trump First and the Presentation of the Political Self." *Anthropology News* 59(2): e145–e148. doi:10.1111/AN.789

8. Davis, Julie Hirschfeld, and Sheryl Gay Stolberg. 2018, January 9. "Trump Appears to Endorse Path to Citizenship for Millions of Immigrants." *New York Times*. https://nyti.ms/2EquDHH

9. The White House. 2018, January 9. "President Trump Meets with Bipartisan Members of the Senate on Immigration." www.youtube.com/watch?v=fc5tIKFDyis&feature=youtu.be&t=35m3s

10. Hulse, Carl. 2018, January 19. "Inside the Oval Office Immigration Meeting That Left a Senator Stunned." *New York Times.* https://nyti.ms/2Dl3k11

11. Rucker, Philip, Sean Sullivan, and Paul Kane. 2017, October 23. "The Great Dealmaker? Lawmakers Find Trump to Be an Untrustworthy Negotiator." *Washington Post.* http://wapo.st/2yHOS1V

12. Duranti, Alessandro. 2006. "Narrating the Political Self in a Campaign for the U.S. Congress." *Language in Society* 35(4): 467–97.

13. Lempert, Michael. 2009. "On 'Flip-Flopping': Branded Stance-Taking in U.S. Electoral Politics." *Journal of Sociolinguistics* 13(2): 223–48.

14. Landler, Mark, and Michael D. Shear. 2018, February 17. "Indictment Makes Trump's Hoax Claim Harder to Sell." *New York Times.* https://nyti.ms/2C1F1Iv

15. Karl, Jonathan. 2017, November 5. "Trump Says Stock Market High 'Because of Me.'" *ABC News.* http://abcn.ws/2zyqsv0

16. Campbell, W. Keith, and Constantine Sedikides. 1999. "Self-Threat Magnifies the Self-Serving Bias: A Meta-Analytic Integration." *Review of General Psychology* 3(1): 23–43.

17. Davis, Julie Hirschfeld, Sheryl Gay Stolberg, and Thomas Kaplan. 2018, January 18. "Trump Was Not 'Fully Informed' in Campaign Vows on Wall, Chief of Staff Says." *New York Times.* https://nyti.ms/2FKIM3T

18. Duranti, "Narrating the Political Self."

19. Duranti, "Narrating the Political Self."

20. Kaplan, Thomas, and Robert Pear. 2017, May 4. "House Passes Measure to Repeal and Replace the Affordable Care Act." *New York Times.* https://nyti.ms/2pLo7He

21. Hannon, Elliot. 2017, June 13. "Trump Reportedly Calls House GOP Health Care Plan 'Mean,' Urges Senators to Be 'More Generous.'" *Slate.* https://slate.com/news-and-politics/2017/06/trump-calls-the-house-gop-health-care-plan-mean-which-it-is.html

22. Kurtzleban, Danielle. 2017, July 20. "Fact Check: Trump's Confusing Remarks to Senate Republicans on Health Care." *National Public Radio.* https://n.pr/2vDnX4g

23. *Reuters.* 2017, July 19. "Inside Trump's Last-Gasp Effort to Save Senate Healthcare Overhaul." http://reut.rs/2uEHy75

24. This essay first appeared in *Anthropology News.* Hodges, Adam. 2017. "Wrestling with 'The Donald.'" *Anthropology News* 58(5): e208–e213. doi:10.1111/AN.593

25. Grunwald, Michael. 2016, July 17. "Donald Trump's One Unbreakable Policy: Skip the Details." *Politico.* www.politico.com/magazine/story/2016/07/donald-trump-policy-2016-hillary-clinton-214058

26. Hall, Goldstein, and Ingram, "Hands of Donald Trump."

27. Bakhtin, Mikhail. 1984. *Rabelais and His World.* Bloomington: Indiana University Press.

28. Smith, Tyson. 2006. "Wrestling with 'Kayfabe.'" *Contexts* 5(2): 54.

29. Shoemaker, David. 2014. *The Squared Circle: Life, Death, and Professional Wrestling.* London: Penguin Books.

30. Stodden, William P., and John S. Hansen. 2017. "Politics by Kayfabe: Professional Wrestling and the Creation of Public Opinion." In *The Sociology of Sports*, Brandon Lang (ed.). San Diego: Cognella.

31. Rogers, Nick. 2017, April 25. "How Wrestling Explains Alex Jones and Donald Trump." *New York Times.* https://nyti.ms/2q1X9sz

32. Barthes, Roland. 1957. *Mythologies.* Paris: Editions du Seuil.

33. Stodden and Hansen, "Politics by Kayfabe."

SECTION 4: RESPONSIBILITY AND DENIABILITY

1. The White House. 2017, October 16. "Remarks by President Trump and Senate Majority Leader Mitch McConnell in

Joint Press Conference." www.whitehouse.gov/briefings-state
ments/remarks-president-trump-senate-majority-leader-mitch
-mcconnell-joint-press-conference/

2. This essay first appeared in *Anthropology News*. Hodges,
Adam. 2017. "Responsibility and Evidence in Trumpian Discourse." *Anthropology News* 58(6): e239–e243. doi:10.1111/AN.676

3. Boas, Franz. 2013 [1911]. *Handbook of American Indian
Languages*. Cambridge: Cambridge University Press.

4. Boas, Franz. 2017 [1938]. *General Anthropology*. London:
Forgotten Books.

5. Fox, Barbara A. 2001. "Evidentiality: Authority, Responsibility, and Entitlement in English Conversation." *Journal of
Linguistic Anthropology* 11(2): 167–92.

6. Aikhenvald, Alexandra. 2004. *Evidentiality*. New York:
Oxford University Press, 5.

7. Blow, Charles. 2018, January 20. "Trump Isn't Hitler: But
the Lying . . . " *New York Times*. https://nyti.ms/2zlXjPA

8. Johnson, Jenna. 2016, June 13. "'A Lot of People Are Saying . . . ': How Trump Spreads Conspiracies and Innuendoes."
Washington Post. http://wapo.st/1XTiBhn

9. This essay first appeared in *Anthropology News*. Hodges,
Adam. 2017. "How Plausibly Deniable Is It?" *Anthropology
News* 58(1): e211–e215. doi:10.1111/AN.335

10. Hall, Kira, Donna Meryl Goldstein, and Matthew Bruce
Ingram. 2016. "The Hands of Donald Trump: Entertainment, Gesture, Spectacle." *HAU: Journal of Ethnographic Theory* 6(2): 71–100.

11. Grice, H. P. 1975. "Logic and Conversation." In *Syntax
and Semantics, Volume 3: Speech Acts*, P. Cole and J. L. Morgan
(eds.). New York: Academic Press.

12. Reddy, Michael. 1979. "The Conduit Metaphor: A Case
of Frame Conflict in Our Language about Language." In *Metaphor and Thought*, Andrew Ortony (ed.), 284–324. Cambridge:
Cambridge University Press.

13. "A Taxonomy of Trump Tweets." 2018, December 1. "On the Media," *WNYC*. www.wnyc.org/story/taxonomy-trump -tweets/

14. Brooks, David. 2018, January 20. "The Lord of Misrule." *New York Times*. https://nyti.ms/2jTkuZN

SECTION 5: THE PROPAGATION OF CONSPIRACY THEORIES

1. This essay first appeared in *Anthropology News*. Hodges, Adam. 2017. "Playing Telephone with the Power of the Presidency." *Anthropology News* 58(2): e214–e218. doi:10.1111/AN.398

2. Bourdieu, Pierre. 1991. *Language and Symbolic Power*, John B. Thompson (ed.), Gino Raymond and Matthew Adamson (trans.). Cambridge, MA: Harvard University Press, 109. Emphasis in these quotations are in the original.

3. Irvine, Judith. 1989. "When Talk Isn't Cheap: Language and Political Economy," *American Ethnologist* 16(2): 248–67.

4. Putnam, Hilary. 1975. "The Meaning of Meaning." In *Mind, Language and Reality: Philosophical Papers 2*, H. Putnam (ed.), 215–71. Cambridge: Cambridge University Press, 228.

5. Emphasis in original.

6. Hodges, Adam. 2011. *The "War on Terror" Narrative: Discourse and Intertextuality in the Construction and Contestation of Sociopolitical Reality.* New York: Oxford University Press.

7. Davis, Julie Hirschfeld. 2017, March 13. "Using Air Quotes, White House Walks Back 'Wiretap' Talk." *New York Times*. https://nyti.ms/2ngbRy4

8. This essay first appeared in *Anthropology News*. Hodges, Adam. 2017. "The Paranoid Style of Climate Change Denial." *Anthropology News* 58(5): e214–e219. doi:10.1111/AN.640

9. Mann, Michael E. 2017, August 28. "It's a Fact: Climate Change Made Hurricane Harvey More Deadly." *The Guardian*.

www.theguardian.com/commentisfree/2017/aug/28/climate-change-hurricane-harvey-more-deadly

10. Diaz, Daniella. 2017, September 8. "EPA Chief on Irma: Not Time to Talk Climate Change." *CNN*. www.cnn.com/2017/09/07/politics/scott-pruitt-hurricanes-climate-change-interview/index.html

11. Hofstadter, Richard. 2008 [1964]. *The Paranoid Style in American Politics, and Other Essays.* New York: Vintage Books, 3.

12. Hofstadter, *Paranoid Style in American Politics*, 29 (emphasis in original).

13. Inhofe, James. 2012. *The Greatest Hoax: How the Global Warming Conspiracy Threatens Your Future.* Washington, DC: WND Books.

14. Lahsen, Myanna. 1999. "The Detection and Attribution of Conspiracies: The Controversy over Chapter 8." In *Paranoia within Reason: A Casebook on Conspiracy as Explanation*, George E. Marcus (ed.), 111–36. Chicago: University of Chicago Press, 114. See also: Lahsen, Myanna. 2013. "Anatomy of Dissent: A Cultural Analysis of Climate Skepticism." *American Behavioral Scientist* 57(6): 732–53.

15. Jones, Alex. 2017, September 13. "Geoengineering Scientists Are Able to Beam Energy from Space to Earth's Surface." *InfoWars*. www.infowars.com/geoengineering-scientists-are-able-to-beam-energy-from-space-to-earths-surface/

16. Hofstadter, *Paranoid Style in American Politics.*

17. Starbird, Kate. 2017, March 15. "Information Wars: A Window into the Alternative Media Ecosystem." *Medium*. https://medium.com/hci-design-at-uw/information-wars-a-window-into-the-alternative-media-ecosystem-a1347f32fd8f

18. Jones, Alex. 2017, September 12. "Hurricanes Are Powered by Electrical Currents in the Ionosphere, Not Warm Water." *InfoWars*. http://newsvideo.su/video/7562482

19. boyd, danah. 2017, January 5. "Did Media Literacy Backfire?" *Data and Society*. https://points.datasociety.net/did -media-literacy-backfire-7418c084d88d

20. Oreskes, Naomi, and Erik M. Conway. 2010. *Merchants of Doubt: How a Handful of Scientists Obscured the Truth on Issues from Tobacco Smoke to Global Warming*. New York: Bloomsbury Press, 18.

21. Walker, Jesse. 2014. *The United States of Paranoia: A Conspiracy Theory*. New York: HarperCollins. Emphasis in original.

22. Oreskes and Conway, *Merchants of Doubt*, 34.

23. Hodges, Adam. 2015. "The Paranoid Style in Politics." *Journal of Language Aggression and Conflict* 3(1): 87–106.

24. This essay first appeared in *Anthropology News*. Hodges, Adam. 2018. "A Theory of Propaganda for the Social Media Age." *Anthropology News* 59(2): e149–e152. doi:10.1111/AN.823

25. Oddo, John. 2018. *The Discourse of Propaganda: Case Studies from the Persian Gulf War and the War on Terror*. University Park: Penn State University Press.

26. Urban, Greg. 1996. "Entextualization, Replication, and Power." In *Natural Histories of Discourse*, Michael Silverstein and Greg Urban (eds.), 21–44. Chicago: University of Chicago Press, 24.

27. Bauman, Richard, and Charles L. Briggs. 1990. "Poetics and Performances as Critical Perspectives on Language and Social Life." *Annual Review of Anthropology* 19(1): 59–88, 73.

28. Griffith, Erin. 2018, February 15. "Pro-Gun Russian Bots Flood Twitter after Parkland Shooting." *Wired*. www.wired .com/story/pro-gun-russian-bots-flood-twitter-after-parkland -shooting/

29. Smiley, Lauren. 2017, November 1. "The College Kids Doing What Twitter Won't." *Wired*. www.wired.com/story/the -college-kids-doing-what-twitter-wont/

30. Spitulnik, Debra. 1996. "The Social Circulation of Media Discourse and the Mediation of Communities." *Journal of Linguistic Anthropology* 6(2): 161–87, 164.

31. Shane, Scott. 2018, February 8. "How Unwitting Americans Encountered Russian Operatives Online." *New York Times.* https://nyti.ms/2C5LodP

32. Apuzzo, Matt, and Sharon LaFraniere. 2018, February 16. "13 Russians Indicted as Mueller Reveals Effort to Aid Trump Campaign." *New York Times.* https://nyti.ms/2C6XKm6

33. Ohlheiser, Abby. 2018, February 22. "Algorithms Are One Reason a Conspiracy Theory Goes Viral: Another Reason Might Be You." *Washington Post.* http://wapo.st/2otyflw

SECTION 6: FAKE NEWS AND MISINFORMATION

1. "Fake news." n.d. *Collins Dictionary.* www.collinsdictionary .com/dictionary/english/fake-news

2. This essay first appeared in *Anthropology News.* Hodges, Adam. 2018. "How 'Fake News' Lost Its Meaning." *Anthropology News* 59(3): e162–e165. doi:10.1111/AN.880

3. "'Fake News' Threat to Media: Editorial Decisions, Outside Actors at Fault." 2018, April 2. Monmouth University Polling Institute. www.monmouth.edu/polling-institute/reports/monmouthpoll_us_040218/

4. This essay first appeared in *Anthropology News.* Hodges, Adam. 2018. "How to Counter Misinformation." *Anthropology News* 59(4): e263–e266. doi:10.1111/AN.899

5. Cook, John, Ullrich Ecker, and Stephan Lewandowsky. 2015. "Misinformation and How to Correct It." In *Emerging Trends in the Social and Behavioral Sciences*, Robert A. Scott and Stephan M. Kosslyn (eds.), 1–17. Hoboken, NJ: Wiley; Schwarz, Norbert, Eryn Newman, and William Leach. 2016. "Making the Truth Stick and the Myths Fade: Lessons from Cognitive Psychology." *Behavioral Science and Policy* 2(1): 85–95.

6. Sullivan, Margaret. 2018, June 17. "Instead of Trump's Propaganda, How About a Nice 'Truth Sandwich'?" *Washington Post*. https://wapo.st/2larıln

7. Cook, John. 2015, June 1. "Making Sense of Climate Science Denial: Sticky Science." www.youtube.com/watch?v=TM-zNOo2phw&feature=youtu.be

8. Hart, P. Sol, and Erik C. Nisbet. 2012. "Boomerang Effects in Science Communication: How Motivated Reasoning and Identity Cues Amplify Opinion Polarization about Climate Mitigation Policies." *Communication Research* 39(6): 701–23.

9. Nyhan, Brendan, and Jason Reifler. 2010. "When Corrections Fail: The Persistence of Political Misperceptions." *Political Behavior* 32(2): 303–30.

10. Cook, John, Stephan Lewandowsky, and Ullrich K. H. Ecker. 2017. "Neutralizing Misinformation through Inoculation: Exposing Misleading Argumentation Techniques Reduces Their Influence." *PLOS ONE* 12(5): e0175799. https://doi.org/10.1371/journal.pone.0175799

11. Cook, Ecker, and Lewandowsky, "Misinformation and How to Correct It."

12. Rizzo, Salvador. 2018, June 19. "The Facts about Trump's Policy of Separating Families at the Border." *Washington Post*. https://wapo.st/2IorQGr

13. Cook, Ecker, and Lewandowsky, "Misinformation and How to Correct It." Emphasis in original

14. Cook, Ecker, and Lewandowsky, "Misinformation and How to Correct It."

SECTION 7: TRUMP AND TERRORISM

1. Bucholtz, Mary, and Kira Hall. 2005. "Identity and Interaction: A Sociocultural Linguistic Approach." *Discourse Studies* 7(4–5): 585–614.

2. Hodges, Adam. 2011. *The "War on Terror" Narrative: Discourse and Intertextuality in the Construction and Contestation of Sociopolitical Reality.* New York: Oxford University Press.

3. This essay first appeared in *Anthropology News.* Hodges, Adam. 2017. "Trump Echoes Bush in Middle East Visit." *Anthropology News* 58(3): e299–e303. doi:10.1111/AN.419

4. The White House. 2017, May 21. "President Trump's Speech to the Arab Islamic American Summit." www.whitehouse.gov/briefings-statements/president-trumps-speech-arab-islamic-american-summit/

5. Trump, Donald J. 2017, May 21. "President Trump's Full Speech from Saudi Arabia on Global Terrorism." *Washington Post.* https://wapo.st/2q9q7Wn

6. Baker, Peter, and Michael D. Shear. 2017, May 21. "Trump Softens Tone on Islam but Calls for Purge of 'Foot Soldiers of Evil.'" *New York Times.* https://nyti.ms/2rFfPyj

7. George W. Bush White House. n.d. "Backgrounder: The President's Quotes on Islam." https://georgewbush-whitehouse.archives.gov/infocus/ramadan/islam.html

8. Hodges, *"War on Terror" Narrative.*

9. Lazar, Annita, and Michelle M. Lazar. 2004. "The Discourse of the New World Order: 'Out-Casting' the Double Face of Threat." *Discourse and Society* 15(2–3): 223–42.

10. The White House. 2017, May 23. "Remarks by President Trump and President Abbas of the Palestinian Authority in Joint Statements." www.whitehouse.gov/briefings-statements/remarks-president-trump-president-abbas-palestinian-authority-joint-statements/

11. Donald J. Trump White House. 2017, January 20. "The Inaugural Address." www.whitehouse.gov/briefings-statements/the-inaugural-address/

12. This essay first appeared in *Anthropology News.* Hodges, Adam. 2018. "Reclaiming 'Allahu Akbar' from Semantic Pejoration." *Anthropology News* 59(4): e267–e272. doi:10.1111/AN.934

13. Mueller, Benjamin, William K. Rashbaum, and Al Baker. 2017, October 31. "Terror Attack Kills 8 and Injures 11 in Manhattan." *New York Times.* https://nyti.ms/2iPvM5M

14. Eckert, Penelope. 2008. "Variation and the Indexical Field." *Journal of Sociolinguistics* 12(4): 453–76.

15. Khan, Ahsan M. 2017, November 1. "Reclaiming 'Allahu Akbar' from Its Misuse by Terrorists." *Los Angeles Times.* www.latimes.com/opinion/readersreact/la-ol-le-new-york-attack-allahu-akbar-20171101-story.html

16. Ali, Wajahat. 2017, November. "I Want 'Allahu Akbar' Back." *New York Times.* https://nyti.ms/2z5bMjR

SECTION 8: RACISM AND WHITE NATIONALISM

1. Coates, Ta-Nehisi. 2017, October. "The First White President." *The Atlantic.* www.theatlantic.com/magazine/archive/2017/10/the-first-white-president-ta-nehisi-coates/537909/

2. This essay first appeared in *Anthropology News.* Hodges, Adam. 2017. "America's Most Consequential Racial Divide." *Anthropology News* 58(4): e278–e281. doi:10.1111/AN.453

3. *New York Times.* 2016, October 5. "Transcript of the 2016 Debate between the Running Mates." https://nyti.ms/2dvSFoz

4. Hill, Jane. 2008. *The Everyday Language of White Racism.* Malden, MA: Wiley-Blackwell.

5. Keneally, Meghan. 2014, November 25. "Exclusive: Darren Wilson Explains How He Feared for His Life." *ABC News.* http://abcn.ws/1yU1LPc

6. Sanburn, Josh. 2016, July 9. "Philando Castile Shooting Had 'Nothing to Do with Race,' Officer's Attorney Says." *Time.* http://time.com/4399926/philando-castile-shooting-jeronimo-yanez/

7. Coates, Ta-Nehisi. 2015. *Between the World and Me.* New York: Spiegel & Grau, 97.

8. Eberhardt, Jennifer L., Phillip Atiba Goff, Valerie J. Purdie, and Paul G. Davies. 2004. "Seeing Black: Race, Crime,

and Visual Processing." *Journal of Personality and Social Psychology* 87(6): 876–93.

9. Mills, Charles. 2008. "White Ignorance." In *Agnotology: The Making and Unmaking of Ignorance*, Robert Proctor and Londa L. Schiebinger (eds.), 230–49. Stanford: Stanford University Press.

10. This essay first appeared in *Anthropology News*. Hodges, Adam. 2018. "White Racism in the White House." *Anthropology News* 59(1): e193–e196. doi:10.1111/AN.768

11. Leonhardt, David, and Ian Prasad Philbrick. 2018, January 15. "Donald Trump's Racism: The Definitive List." *The New York Times*. https://nyti.ms/2EKws1Z.

12. Davis, Julie Hirschfeld, Sheryl Gay Stolberg, and Thomas Kaplan. 2018, January 11. "Trump Alarms Lawmakers with Disparaging Words for Haiti and Africa." *New York Times*. https://nyti.ms/2EzkEQe

13. Hill, *Everyday Language of White Racism*.

14. Hodges, Adam. 2015. "Ideologies of Language and Race in US Media Discourse about the Trayvon Martin Shooting." *Language in Society* 44(3): 401–23; Hodges, Adam. 2016. "Accusatory and Exculpatory Moves in the Hunting for 'Racists' Language Game." *Language and Communication* 47: 1–14; Hodges, Adam. 2016. "Hunting for 'Racists': Tape Fetishism and the Intertextual Enactment and Reproduction of the Dominant Understanding of Racism in US Society." *Journal of Linguistic Anthropology* 26(1): 26–40.

15. Bonilla-Silva, Eduardo. 2013. *Racism without Racists: Color-Blind Racism and the Persistence of Racial Inequality in America*. Plymouth, UK: Rowman & Littlefield.

16. Wittgenstein, Ludwig. 1953. *Philosophical Investigations*. Malden, MA: Wiley-Blackwell.

17. Bonilla-Silva, *Racism without Racists*.

18. Hill, *Everyday Language of White Racism*.

19. Davis, Julie Hirschfeld. 2018, January 12. "A Senior Republican Senator Admonishes Trump: 'America Is an Idea, Not a Race.'" *New York Times*. https://nyti.ms/2FrwgG9

20. Johnson, Jenna, Vanessa Williams, and Marc Fisher. 2018, January 12. "Trump's Vulgarity: Overt Racism or a President Who Says What Many Think?" *Washington Post*. http://wapo.st/2D5N34d

21. This essay first appeared in *Anthropology News*. Hodges, Adam. 2018. "What 'Types of Racism' Does Trump Recognize?" *Anthropology News* 59(5): e163–e166. doi:10.1111/AN.959

22. Boas, Franz. 1912. "Changes in the Bodily Form of Descendants of Immigrants." *American Anthropologist* 14(3): 530–62.

23. Sears, David O., and P. J. Henry. 2005. "Over Thirty Years Later: A Contemporary Look at Symbolic Racism." *Advances in Experimental Social Psychology* 37: 95–150; Tarman, Christopher, and David O. Sears. 2005. "The Conceptualization and Measurement of Symbolic Racism." *Journal of Politics* 67(3): 731–61.

24. Bob, Lawrence, James R. Kluegel, and Ryan A. Smith. 1997. "Laissez-faire Racism: The Crystallization of a Kinder, Gentler, Antiblack Ideology." In *Racial Attitudes in the 1990s*, Steven A. Tuch and Jack K. Martin (eds.), 15–42. London: Praeger.

25. Dovidio, John F., and Samuel L. Gaertner. 2004. "Aversive Racism." *Advances in Experimental Social Psychology* 36: 1–52.

26. Hill, *Everyday Language of White Racism*.

27. Feagin, Joe R. 2006. *Systemic Racism: A Theory of Oppression*. New York: Routledge.

28. Bonilla-Silva, *Racism without Racists*.

29. Coates, Ta-Nehisi. 2014, May 21. "The Case for Reparations." *The Atlantic*. www.theatlantic.com/features/archive/2014/05/the-case-for-reparations/361631/

30. Ansell, Amy Elizabeth. 2013. *Race and Ethnicity: The Key Concepts*. New York: Routledge.

31. Spanierman, Lisa B., and Nolan L. Cabrera. 2014. "The Emotions of White Racism and Antiracism." In *Unveiling Whiteness in the Twenty-First Century: Global Manifestations, Transdisciplinary Interventions*, Veronica Watson, Deirdre Howard-Wagner, and Lisa Spanierman (eds.), 9–28. Lanham, MD: Lexington Books, 16.

SECTION 9: POLITICAL RESISTANCE

1. This essay first appeared in *Anthropology News*. Hodges, Adam. 2017. "Rescuing Ourselves from the Argument Culture." *Anthropology News* 58(6): e244–e249. doi:10.1111/AN.712

2. Vazquez, Maegan. 2017, October 24. "Trump-Corker Feud Explodes ahead of Critical Hill Visit." *CNN*. www.cnn.com/2017/10/24/politics/corker-trump-photo-op-tax-plan/index.html

3. Flake, Jeff. 2017, October 24. "Full Transcript: Jeff Flake's Speech on the Senate Floor." *New York Times*. https://nyti.ms/2h6rhQA

4. Wagner, John, and Scott Clement. 2017, October 28. "'It's Just Messed Up': Most Say Political Divisions Are as Bad as in Vietnam War Era, Poll Shows." *Washington Post*. http://wapo.st/2zdBMwn

5. Kamenetz, Anya. 2017, October 26. "Teachers Report Stressed, Anxious Students in the 'Age of Trump.'" *National Public Radio*. https://n.pr/2yHxFI8

6. Tannen, Deborah. 1999. *The Argument Culture*. New York: Penguin Random House.

7. Tannen, Deborah. 2013. "The Argument Culture: Agonism & the Common Good." *Dædalus* 142(2): 177–84.

8. Foucault, Michel. 2004. *Society Must Be Defended: Lectures at the Collège de France, 1975–76*. New York: Penguin.

9. Lee, Jasmine C., and Kevin Quealy. 2016, January 28. "The People, Places and Things Donald Trump Has Insulted on Twitter: A Complete List." *New York Times.* https://nyti.ms/2jRpoL3

10. Edkins, Brett. 2016, December 13. "Study: Trump Benefited from 'Overwhelmingly Negative' Tone of Election News Coverage." *Forbes.* www.forbes.com/sites/brettedkins/2016/12/13/trump-benefited-from-overwhelmingly-negative-tone-of-election-news-coverage-study-finds/; *Fortune.* 2016, December 9. "How Much Less than Hillary Clinton Donald Trump Spent on the Election." http://fortune.com/2016/12/09/hillary-clinton-donald-trump-campaign-spending/

11. Patterson, Thomas E. 2016, December 7. "News Coverage of the 2016 General Election: How the Press Failed the Voters." Harvard University Shorenstein Center on Media, Politics and Public Policy. https://shorensteincenter.org/news-coverage-2016-general-election/

12. Ratcliffe, Krista. 2005. *Rhetorical Listening: Identification, Gender, Whiteness.* Carbondale: Southern Illinois University Press.

13. Foss, Sonja K., and Cindy L. Griffin. 1995. "Beyond Persuasion: A Proposal for an Invitational Rhetoric." *Communication Monographs* 62(1): 2–18.

14. Young, Richard Emerson, Alton L. Becker, and Kenneth Lee Pike. 1970. *Rhetoric: Discovery and Change.* New York: Harcourt, Brace & World.

15. Lunsford, Andrea A., and John J. Ruszkiewicz. 2015. *Everything's an Argument.* London: Macmillan.

16. Noah, Trevor. 2017, October 16. "Get with The Times: Trevor Noah and John Eligon." *New York Times.* www.youtube.com/watch?v=31k4Lg794Pk&feature=youtu.be&t=46m50s

17. The White House. 2017, June 29. "Press Briefing by Principal Deputy Press Secretary Sarah Sanders and Treasury Secretary Mnuchin." www.whitehouse.gov/briefings-statements/press-briefing-principal-deputy-press-secretary-sarah-sanders-treasury-secretary-mnuchin-062917/

18. Merica, Dan. 2017, October 24. "Trump Warns McCain: 'Be Careful Because at Some Point I Fight Back.'" *CNN*. www.cnn .com/2017/10/17/politics/trump-john-mccain-feud/index.html

19. This essay first appeared in *Anthropology News*. Hodges, Adam. 2018. "#MeToo Holds Lessons for Political Resistance." *Anthropology News* 59(3): e157–e161. doi:10.1111/AN.857

20. Ponsot, Elisabeth, and Sarah Slobin. 2017, November 17. "17 Women Have Accused Trump of Sexual Misconduct: It's Time to Revisit Those Stories." *Quartz*. https://qz.com/1130324/ 17-women-have-accused-donald-trump-of-sexual-assault-or -misconduct-its-time-to-revisit-those-stories/

21. Parker, Ashley, and Amy Chozick. 2016, October 22. "Donald Trump Pledges to 'Heal Divisions' (and Sue His Accusers)." *New York Times*. https://nyti.ms/2es4U8k

22. Blake, Aaron. 2017, March 8. "21 Times Donald Trump Has Assured Us He Respects Women." *Washington Post*. https:// wapo.st/2mAUNlo

23. DelReal, Jose. 2016, October 14. "Trump Mocks Sexual Assault Accuser: 'She Would Not Be My First Choice.'" *Washington Post*. https://wapo.st/2dpROa4

24. Hackett, Larry. 2016, October 14. "I Edited the People Writer Who Says Trump Groped Her: Here's Why She Didn't Speak Out." *Washington Post*. http://wapo.st/2eAR1oU

25. Hsu, Hua. 2016, November 13. "What Normalization Means." *New Yorker*. www.newyorker.com/culture/cultural-comment/what-normalization-means

26. Bates, Laura. 2017, January 13. "It's Not Groping or Fondling—It Is Sexual Assault." *The Guardian*. www.theguardian .com/lifeandstyle/2017/jan/13/its-not-groping-or-fondling-it -is-sexual-assault

27. Graham, David A. 2017, November 13. "Mitch McConnell on Roy Moore: 'I Believe the Women, Yes.'" *The Atlantic*. www.theatlantic.com/politics/archive/2017/11/i-believe-the -women-yes/545750/

28. Buchanan, Larry, Alicia Parlapiano, and Karen Yourish. 2016, October 10. "Paul Ryan and Mitch McConnell Reject Donald Trump's Words, Over and Over, but Not His Candidacy." *New York Times.* https://nyti.ms/2ntw9Us

29. This essay first appeared in *Anthropology News.* Hodges, Adam. 2018. "Speaking with Silence." *Anthropology News* 59(5): e167–e170. doi:10.1111/AN.1006

30. Basso, Keith. 1970. "'To Give Up on Words': Silence in Western Apache Culture." *Southwestern Journal of Anthropology* 26(3): 213–30, 215.

31. Jaworski, Adam. 1997. *Silence: Interdisciplinary Perspectives.* Berlin: Walter de Gruyter; Tannen, Deborah, and Muriel Saville-Troike (eds.). 1985. *Perspectives on Silence.* New York: Ablex.

32. Tannen, Deborah. 1990. "Silence as Conflict Management in Fiction and Drama." In *Conflict Talk: Sociolinguistic Investigations of Arguments in Conversations*, Allen Grimshaw (ed.), 260–79. Cambridge: Cambridge University Press.

33. Tannen, Deborah. 1985. "Silence: Anything But." In *Perspectives on Silence*, Deborah Tannen and Muriel Saville-Troike (eds.), 93–111. New York: Ablex, 94.

34. Jaworski, Adam. 1998. "The Silence of Power and Solidarity in Fallen Sons." *Studia Anglica Posnaniensia*, 33: 141–52.

35. Foucault, Michel. 2012 [1978]. *The History of Sexuality: An Introduction.* New York: Knopf Doubleday, 101.

36. Trester, Anna Marie. 2013. "Performing Peace." In *Discourses of War and Peace*, Adam Hodges (ed.), 225–45. New York: Oxford University Press.

37. Kunreuther, Laura. 2018. "Sounds of Democracy: Performance, Protest, and Political Subjectivity." *Cultural Anthropology* 33(1): 1–31.

38. Hoffman, Benjamin, and Talya Minsberg. 2018, September 4. "The Deafening Silence of Colin Kaepernick." *New York Times.* https://nyti.ms/2Cel95U

39. Schoeller, Martin. 2017, November 13. "Colin Kaepernick Will Not Be Silenced." *GQ*. www.gq.com/story/colin-kaepernick-will-not-be-silenced

40. Williams, Chad. 2017, July 28. "A Century Later, the First Mass African-American Protest Remains Shamefully Relevant." *Newsweek*. www.newsweek.com/black-lives-matter-silent-protest-parade-first-mass-african-american-642322

41. Kaepernick, Colin. 2018, April 21. "Transcript of Speech: Amnesty International's Ambassador of Conscience Award." Amnesty International. www.amnesty.nl/content/uploads/2018/04/Colin-Kaepernicks-Speech-Ambassador-of-Conscience-Final.pdf

42. Grynbaum, Michael M. 2018, September 13. "Under Fire, Robert Mueller Has a Novel P.R. Strategy: Silence." *New York Times*. https://nyti.ms/2Mr5e3S

SECTION 10: SUPREME COURT POLITICS

1. This essay first appeared in *Anthropology News*. Hodges, Adam. 2017. "The Myth of the Apolitical Judge: How Language Ideologies Underlie the Judicial Confirmation Process." *Anthropology News* 58(3): e294–e298. doi:10.1111/AN.419

2. Philips, Susan. 1998. *Ideology in the Language of Judges*. New York: Oxford University Press.

3. Confirmation Hearing on the Nomination of Hon. Neil M. Gorsuch to be an Associate Justice of the Supreme Court of the United States. 2017. Senate, 115th Congress. www.govinfo.gov/content/pkg/CHRG-115shrg28638/pdf/CHRG-115shrg28638.pdf

4. Confirmation Hearing on the Nomination of John G. Roberts, Jr. to be Chief Justice of the United States. 2017. Senate, 115th Congress. www.govinfo.gov/content/pkg/GPO-CHRG-ROBERTS/pdf/GPO-CHRG-ROBERTS.pdf

5. Hobbs, Pamela. 2011. "Defining the Law: (Mis)Using the Dictionary to Decide Cases." *Discourse Studies* 13(3): 327–47.

6. Solan, Lawrence. 1993. *The Language of Judges*. Chicago: University of Chicago Press.

7. Thompson, John. 1990. *Ideology and Modern Culture*. Oxford: Polity Press.

8. Blommaert, Jan. 2005. *Discourse: A Critical Introduction*. Cambridge: Cambridge University Press, 185.

9. Silverstein, Michael. 1979. "Language Structure and Linguistic Ideology." In *The Elements: A Parasession on Linguistic Units and Levels*, Paul R. Clyne, William F. Hanks, and Carol L. Hofbauer (eds.), 193–247. Chicago: Chicago Linguistic Society.

10. Reddy, Michael. 1979. "The Conduit Metaphor." In *Metaphor and Thought*, Andrew Ortony (ed.), 284–324. Cambridge: Cambridge University Press.

11. Confirmation Hearing on the Nomination of John G. Roberts, Jr. to be Chief Justice of the United States. 2017. Senate, 115th Congress. www.govinfo.gov/content/pkg/GPO-CHRG-ROBERTS/pdf/GPO-CHRG-ROBERTS.pdf

12. The Nomination of Elena Kagan to be an Associate Justice of the Supreme Court of the United States. 2010. Senate, 111th Congress. http://purl.fdlp.gov/GPO/gpo12385

13. Wimsatt, William K., and Monroe C. Beardsley. 1954. *Verbal Icon Studies in the Meaning of Poetry*. Lexington: University of Kentucky Press.

14. Duranti, Alessandro. 1993. "Truth and Intentionality: An Ethnographic Critique." *Cultural Anthropology* 8(2): 214–45; Hill, Jane. 2008. *The Everyday Language of White Racism*. Malden, MA: Wiley-Blackwell; Rosaldo, Michelle. 1982. "The Things We Do with Words: Ilongot Speech Acts and Speech Act Theory in Philosophy." *Language in Society* 11(2): 203–37.

15. Nomination of Ruth Bader Ginsburg to be Associate Justice of the Supreme Court of the United States. 1993. Senate, 103rd Congress. www.govinfo.gov/content/pkg/GPO-CHRG-GINSBURG/pdf/GPO-CHRG-GINSBURG.pdf

16. Hill, *Everyday Language of White Racism*, 38.

17. Nomination of Judge Antonin Scalia to be Associate Justice of the Supreme Court of the United States. 1986. Senate, 99th Congress. www.govinfo.gov/content/pkg/GPO-CHRG -SCALIA/pdf/GPO-CHRG-SCALIA.pdf

18. Hill, *Everyday Language of White Racism*, 33.

19. Confirmation Hearing on the Nomination of Hon. Neil M. Gorsuch to be an Associate Justice of the Supreme Court of the United States. 2017. Senate, 115th Congress. www.govinfo.gov/ content/pkg/CHRG-115shrg28638/pdf/CHRG-115shrg28638.pdf

20. Kavanaugh, Brett. 2018, September 4. "Full Text: Brett Kavanaugh Confirmation Hearing Opening Statement." *Politico*. www.politico.com/story/2018/09/04/full-text-brett-kavanaugh -confirmation-hearing-opening-statements-806420

21. Barnes, Robert. 2018, October 4. "Retired Justice Stevens Calls Kavanaugh's Hearing Performance Disqualifying." *Washington Post*. https://wapo.st/2xZkctR

22. "Kavanaugh Hearing Cold Open." 2018, September 29. *Saturday Night Live*. https://www.youtube.com/watch?v=VRJecfRxbr8

23. Schwartz, Alexandra. 2018, September 27. "Brett Kavanaugh and the Adolescent Aggression of Conservative Masculinity." *New Yorker*. www.newyorker.com/news/current/brett-kavanaughs -adolescent-temper-tantrum-before-the-senate-judiciary-committee

24. Sherman, Gabriel. 2018, September 27. "'This Was Why He Nominated Him': Kavanaugh's Raw, Angry, Partisan Performance Got Trump Back on the Bus." *Vanity Fair*. www.vanityfair. com/news/2018/09/kavanaughs-raw-angry-partisan-performance -trump

25. Butler, Judith. 1990. *Gender Trouble: Feminism and the Subversion of Identity*. New York: Routledge, 145. Emphasis in original.

26. Bucholtz, Mary, and Kira Hall. 2005. "Identity and Interaction: A Sociocultural Linguistic Approach." *Discourse Studies* 7(4–5): 585–614, 586.

SECTION 11: MOVING PAST TRUMP

1. This essay first appeared in *Anthropology News*. Hodges, Adam. 2018. "Government Of, By and For the Trolls." *Anthropology News* 59(6). doi:10.1111/AN.1061

2. Donath, Judith S. 1999. "Identity and Deception in the Virtual Community." In *Communities in Cyberspace*, M. A. Smith and P. Kollock (eds.), 29–59. London: Routledge.

3. Herring, Susan, Kirk Job-Sluder, Rebecca Scheckler, and Sasha Barab. 2002. "Searching for Safety Online: Managing 'Trolling' in a Feminist Forum." *The Information Society* 18: 371–84.

4. The White House. 2018, November 20. "Statement from President Donald J. Trump on Standing with Saudi Arabia." www .whitehouse.gov/briefings-statements/statement-president -donald-j-trump-standing-saudi-arabia/

5. Blake, Aaron. 2018, November 19. "3 Takeaways from Trump's Testy Fox News Interview." *Washington Post*. www .washingtonpost.com/politics/2018/11/19/takeaways-trumps -testy-fox-news-interview/

6. Rucker, Philip, Josh Dawsey, and Damian Paletta. 2018, November 27. "Trump Slams Fed Chair, Questions Climate Change and Threatens to Cancel Putin Meeting in Wide-Ranging Interview with the Post." *Washington Post*. https:// wapo.st/2FLjB5e

7. Schmitt, Eric, and Nicholas Fandos. 2018, December 4. "Saudi Prince 'Complicit' in Khashoggi's Murder, Senators Say after C.I.A. Briefing." *New York Times*. https://nyti.ms/2zG4CnK

8. Borenstein, Seth, and Zeke Miller. 2018, November 26. "Trump: 'I don't believe' Government Climate Report Finding." Associated Press. https://apnews.com/c1dfca3088b448d398 ddc27ffa8dedbf

9. Rucker, Dawsey, and Paletta, "Trump Slams Fed Chair."

9 781503 610798